simply LISTENING

12 months with God

Patsy Lewis

BEACON HILL PRESS
OF KANSAS CITY

Cover Design: Darlene Filley
Internal Design: Sharon Page

All Scripture quotations not otherwise designated are from the *Holy Bible, New International Version®* (NIV®). Copyright © 1973, 1978, 1984 by the International Bible Society. Used by permission of Zondervan Publishing House. All rights reserved.

Permission to quote from the following additional copyrighted versions of the Bible is acknowledged with appreciation:

The *Holy Bible, New Living Translation* (NLT), copyright © 1996, 2004. Used by permission of Tyndale House Publishers, Inc., Wheaton, IL 60189. All rights reserved.

The *New Revised Standard Version* (NRSV) of the Bible, copyright 1989 by the Division of Christian Education of the National Council of the Churches of Christ in the USA. All rights reserved.

The Message (TM). Copyright © 1993, 1994, 1995, 1996, 2000, 2001, 2002. Used by permission of NavPress Publishing Group.

Scripture quotations marked KJV are from the King James Version of the Bible.

Library of Congress Cataloging-in-Publication Data

Lewis, Patsy, 1942-
  Simply listening : 12 months with God / Patsy Lewis.
    p. cm.
  Includes bibliographical references (p.   ).
  ISBN 978-0-8341-2441-7 (pbk.)
  1. Devotional calendars. 2. Bible—Meditations. 3. Listening—Religious aspects—Christianity—Meditations. I. Title.

  BV4811.L49 2009
  242'.2—dc22

                                                    2008049944

10 9 8 7 6 5 4 3 2 1

CONTENTS

INTRODUCTION

The Bible is alive; it speaks to me. It has feet;
it runs after me. It has hands; it takes hold of me.[1]
—Martin Luther

My purpose in writing this devotional book is to guide you as you develop ears to hear and an open heart to receive messages from God through scripture and quiet moments alone with Him. Since creation, God has initiated relationship and communication with humanity. He has powerful messages to deliver to you—if you simply listen.

A number of years ago I was inspired by the book *God Calling*[2] to dialogue with God and write down the messages I sensed Him giving to me. Although the messages I received were given to me personally for special situations, I believe it's appropriate to share some of them with you to encourage and inspire you as you listen to what He may be saying to *you*.

The primary way God speaks is through Scripture. That's why it's so important to be in the Word as you ask, *What is God saying to me?* A message that comes from God will never be contrary to the essence of Scripture and God's character.

Simply Listening is designed to be read with your Bible open in your hand as you spend time with Him and listen for what He has to say to you. God created you, and He desires an ongoing relationship with you.

LISTENING TO GOD'S QUESTIONS

God created us for a personal relationship with Him. In the opening chapters of the Old Testament we read that God created humanity in His own image, breathed life into His supreme creation, and was pleased with His creation:

The Lord God formed man from the dust of the ground, and breathed into his nostrils the breath of life; and the man became a living being (*Genesis 2:7*, NRSV).

So God created human beings in his own image. In the image of God he created them; male and female he created them (*Genesis 1:27*, NLT).

God saw all that he had made, and it was very good (*Genesis 1:31*).

Early in Scripture we see God in relationship with humanity. His conversations with His created beings give us insight into His desire for fellowship. The questions He asks, placing Him in control of the conversations and expecting the listener to reply, are intriguing:

"Where are you?" (Genesis 3:9).

"Who told you that you were naked?" (Genesis 3:11).

"Have you eaten from the tree whose fruit I commanded you not to eat?" (Genesis 3:11, NLT).

"What is this you have done?" (Genesis 3:13).

God not only sees our actions; He also expects us to confess them to Him.

God spoke to Cain, the son of Adam and Eve, in Genesis 4. Once again He asked pointed questions, expecting a response and revealing that He's aware of our emotions and what's in our hearts.

To Cain, God asked, "Why are you angry? Why is your face downcast?" (Genesis 4:6).

Cain would have been wise to listen and heed God's advice: "You will be accepted if you do what is right. But if you refuse to do what is right, then watch out! Sin is crouching at the door, eager to control you. But you must subdue it and be its master" (Genesis 4:7, NLT).

After Cain murdered his brother Abel, God continued to question Cain: "Where is your brother Abel?" (Genesis 4:9). "What have you done?" (Genesis 4:10).

God's next word is "Listen!" (Genesis 4:10).

In prayer, an emphasis is often placed on confession, asking, praise, thanksgiving, intercession—the part we ourselves play in the conversation. Listening is frequently neglected or sometimes even ignored.

It's obvious from these conversations in Genesis that God expects us to listen to Him and that disobedience to His instructions is serious and reaps consequences.

It's also clear that God continues conversations even when His creatures disappoint Him.

Cain said to the LORD, "My punishment is more than I can bear. Today you are driving me from the land, and I will be hidden from your presence; I will be a restless wanderer on the earth, and whoever finds me will kill me."

But the LORD said to him, "Not so; if anyone kills Cain, he will suffer vengeance seven times over." Then the LORD put a mark on Cain so that no one who found him would kill him. So Cain went out from the Lord's presence and lived in the land of Nod, east of Eden (*Genesis 4:13-16*).

Might Cain's story have ended differently had he listened and heeded God's warning?

• • • • • •

Our friend's life was spiraling downward. He had once been active in church, serving in leadership roles. Now his marriage was crumbling. He was having an affair with another woman and was rebellious toward God. Months into this lifestyle change, his family had lost hope, and he had no intentions of changing. He tells that one day as he was traveling in his truck, he sensed a voice saying to him, "Don't go down that hill!" He believed this was a divine warning. He turned his truck around, went immediately to the other woman, told her the affair was off, and returned to his wife. Years later, his wife confirmed that he immediately repaired his relationship with God, with his family, and with her. I asked him once if he ever went down that hill.

"Absolutely not—I was afraid to!" he said. This was a man who, unlike Cain, harkened to God's warning.

• • • • • •

Recently in my listening time, after reading the account of Jesus healing the blind man in Luke 18:35-43, I sensed God asking me the precise question he had asked the blind man: "What do you want me to do for you?" (Luke 18:41). That question opened the door for me to pour out my heart to the Lord. I have learned through my listening times that God asks probing questions, gives sound advice, and lets me know that He not only expects obedience but is also waiting to listen to my heart cries and questions.

This month, practice asking and answering questions as you read and pray.

- Asking questions as you read is an excellent retention skill.
- Asking questions during dialogue keeps the conversation alive.
- Asking the question *Are you saying what I think I hear you saying?* helps clarify and aids communication.

Most of the "Listen through Scripture" passages are the words of Jesus. Watch for the questions He asks, and underline them. Probe the depths of your heart to see how you might have answered each question. Ask yourself what emotions Jesus or His listeners might be experiencing. Put yourself into the scene. What would you be feeling?

Do you recall your first conversation with God?

What are some questions God has asked you in the past?

What question is He asking you today?

Listen to and answer God's questions to you.

Respond to questions you read in Scripture.

Ask yourself, *What is this saying to me?*

Following each scripture will be a short reading, "What I sensed God saying to me," that came through my personal listening times over the years. There is then a space to write what you sense God saying to you as you wait quietly in His presence. If you've never practiced listening as a part of your prayer and devotional time, I invite you to start today.

Focus for the Month:

Genesis 1-4

John 1; 5-15

TODAY IS _____

Listen through scripture:

JOHN 1:1-5, NLT:

In the beginning the Word already existed. The Word was with God, and the Word was God. He existed in the beginning with God. God created everything through him, and nothing was created except through him. The Word gave life to everything that was created, and his life brought light to everyone. The light shines in the darkness, and the darkness can never extinguish it.

What I sensed God saying to me:

Face the New Year with confidence and expectation. I will renew your strength for the assignments I give you. The year lies before you like an open book filled with mystery and curiosity as to how it will end. The pages will unfold chapter by chapter, day by day, week by week. I am the God of eternal renewal. The New Year holds new adventures, new insights, new treasures! Explore and hold dear each one as I, the Creator, paint the landscape and details of your journey.

What message is God giving you?

_____

_____

_____

_____

_____

_____

_____

_____

_____

_____

TODAY IS _____

Listen through scripture:

JOHN 5:24 AND 6:40:

I tell you the truth, whoever hears my word and believes him who sent me has eternal life and will not be condemned; he has crossed over from death to life (5:24).

For my Father's will is that everyone who looks to the Son and believes in him shall have eternal life, and I will raise him up at the last day (6:40).

What I sensed God saying to me:

I have given you eternal life. I came to give you abundant life; to reveal truth to you; to set you free from the bondage of sin. Rejoice! Victory is assured.

What message is God giving you?

_____

_____

_____

_____

_____

_____

_____

_____

_____

_____

_____

TODAY IS _____

Listen through scripture:

JOHN 6:35 AND 6:47-48:

> *Then Jesus declared, "I am the bread of life. He who comes to me will never go hungry, and he who believes in me will never be thirsty (6:35).*
>
> *I tell you the truth, he who believes has everlasting life. I am the bread of life (6:47-48).*

What I sensed God saying to me:

> *Come to me just to be near me. I will use you to lead others to the Living Water and to restore hope to the despairing ones and joy to the downhearted.*

What message is God giving you?

_____

_____

_____

_____

_____

_____

_____

_____

_____

_____

_____

_____

TODAY IS _____

Listen through scripture:

JOHN 7:37-39:

> *On the last and greatest day of the Feast, Jesus stood and said in a loud voice, "If anyone is thirsty, let him come to me and drink. Whoever believes in me, as the Scripture has said, streams of living water will flow from within him." By this he meant the Spirit, whom those who believed in him were later to receive. Up to that time the Spirit had not been given, since Jesus had not yet been glorified.*

What I sensed God saying to me:

> *My Spirit lives in you. I am a holy God. Be holy and follow my example. As you seek my face and obey my instructions, you will reflect my holiness.*

What message is God giving you?

_____

_____

_____

_____

_____

_____

_____

_____

_____

_____

_____

TODAY IS _____

Listen through scripture:

JOHN 8:31-32, NLT:

Jesus said to the people who believed in him, "You are truly my disciples if you remain faithful to my teachings. And you will know the truth, and the truth will set you free."

What I sensed God saying to me:

It is my desire for you to be a person of truth in all your dealings. Renounce immediately anything in your spirit that you would be ashamed for others to see—envy, jealousy, selfishness, unkind thoughts.

What message is God giving you?

_____

_____

_____

_____

_____

_____

_____

_____

_____

_____

_____

_____

TODAY IS _____

Listen through scripture:

JOHN 10:27:

My sheep listen to my voice; I know them, and they follow me.

What I sensed God saying to me:

The more you listen for my voice, the easier it will be to recognize it. I want to lead you and your loved ones. You are mine. Look to me, and I will help you have peace.

What message is God giving you?

_____

_____

_____

_____

_____

_____

_____

_____

_____

_____

_____

_____

_____

TODAY IS _____

Listen through scripture:

JOHN 12:25-26, NLT:

Those who love their life in this world will lose it. Those who care nothing for their life in this world will keep it for eternity. Anyone who wants to be my disciple must follow me, because my servants must be where I am. And the Father will honor anyone who serves me.

What I sensed God saying to me:

Follow me. I have led you before. I am sufficient for all your needs. You also found my joy in difficult circumstances. Other times you have followed me down paths that looked rosy but discovered rocky roads and hard times. Look back and see me providing and walking with you through the darkest times. That is why you can follow me confidently, knowing I have been with you in the past, assured that I will walk with you into the unknown.

What message is God giving you?

_____

_____

_____

_____

_____

_____

_____

_____

_____

_____

TODOY IS _____

Listen through scripture:

JOHN 13:12-17:

When he had finished washing their feet, he put on his clothes and returned to his place. "Do you understand what I have done for you?" he asked them. "You call me 'Teacher' and 'Lord,' and rightly so, for that is what I am. Now that I, your Lord and Teacher, have washed your feet, you also should wash one another's feet. I have set you an example that you should do as I have done for you. I tell you the truth, no servant is greater than his master, nor is a messenger greater than the one who sent him. Now that you know these things, you will be blessed if you do them."

What I sensed God saying to me:

I have called you to be my servant. Remain alert for opportunities to love and show a Christlike spirit. Show courtesy to all, even the evil, ill-mannered people you meet. Keep a positive outlook. Look for the good in all people created in my image.

What message is God giving you?

_____

_____

_____

_____

_____

_____

_____

_____

_____

_____

TODAY IS _____

Listen through scripture:

JOHN 14:1:

> *Do not let your hearts be troubled. Trust in God; trust also in me.*

What I sensed God saying to me:

> *Bring your troubled heart to me. Treat today as a holy day, for it is. Sing and pray scripture, and, of course, live it. Each time you feel a gentle breeze or hear the wind blow, think of me, the divine Holy Spirit who lives in you.*

What message is God giving you?

_____

_____

_____

_____

_____

_____

_____

_____

_____

_____

_____

_____

_____

_____

TODAY IS _____

Listen through scripture:

JOHN 14:9-12:

Jesus answered: "Don't you know me, Philip, even after I have been among you such a long time? Anyone who has seen me has seen the Father. How can you say, 'Show us the Father'? Don't you believe that I am in the Father, and that the Father is in me? The words I say to you are not just my own. Rather, it is the Father, living in me, who is doing his work. Believe me when I say that I am in the Father and the Father is in me, or at least believe on the evidence of the miracles themselves. I tell you the truth, anyone who has faith in me will do what I have been doing. He will do even greater things than these, because I am going to the Father."

What I sensed God saying to me:

Your faith will be strengthened. You will see. Listen in silence before me.

What message is God giving you?

_____

_____

_____

_____

_____

_____

_____

_____

_____

_____

TODAY IS _____

Listen through scripture:

JOHN 14:15, 21, 23-24:

> *If you love me, you will obey what I command* (14:15).
>
> *Whoever has my commands and obeys them, he is the one who loves me. He who loves me will be loved by my Father, and I too will love him and show myself to him* (14:21).
>
> *If anyone loves me, he will obey my teaching. My Father will love him, and we will come to him and make our home with him. He who does not love me will not obey my teaching. These words you hear are not my own; they belong to the Father who sent me* (14:23-24).

What I sensed God saying to me:

> *Continue to read the Word prayerfully, probing, digging, listening for truths from me to enlighten your own heart and to share with others. This is how you learn what I desire from you.*

What message is God giving you?

_____

_____

_____

_____

_____

_____

_____

_____

_____

TODAY IS _____

Listen through scripture:

JOHN 14:27:

> *Peace I leave with you; my peace I give you. I do not give to you as the world gives. Do not let your hearts be troubled and do not be afraid.*

What I sensed God saying to me:

> *Breathe in my peace. Give today to me. Be benevolent, friendly, gentle, and kind. I love you even when you aren't perfect. I know and understand your heart. Take my peace with you into your world today.*

What message is God giving you?

_____

_____

_____

_____

_____

_____

_____

_____

_____

_____

_____

_____

_____

TODAY IS _____

Listen through scripture:

JOHN 15:9-11:

> As the Father has loved me, so have I loved you. Now remain in my love. If you obey my commands, you will remain in my love, just as I have obeyed my Father's commands and remain in his love. I have told you this so that my joy may be in you and that your joy may be complete.

What I sensed God saying to me:

> Your word today is joy. Receive my joy and spread it. Do not let any person or any situation rob you of joy.

What message is God giving you?

_____

_____

_____

_____

_____

_____

_____

_____

_____

_____

_____

_____

TODAY IS _____

Listen through scripture:

JOHN 15:16:

You did not choose me, but I chose you and appointed you to go and bear fruit—fruit that will last. Then the Father will give you whatever you ask in my name.

What I sensed God saying to me:

Have you noticed that I often repeat messages to you? Take my words seriously. Keep my face ever before you, and I will fill your mind with guidance and help you control your thoughts, attitudes, and responses. I know the plans I have for you. Don't lose hope or your zeal for my work.

What message is God giving you?

_____

_____

_____

_____

_____

_____

_____

_____

_____

_____

_____

_____

TODAY IS _____

Listen through Scripture:

JOHN 15:17:

> *This is my command: Love each other.*

I JOHN 3:11-12:

> *This is the message you heard from the beginning: We should love one another. Do not be like Cain, who belonged to the evil one and murdered his brother. And why did he murder him? Because his own actions were evil and his brother's were righteous.*

What I sensed God saying to me:

> *Walk with your brothers and sisters in Christ through days of despair and hopelessness. Redirect their thoughts to me. Love each other!*

What message is God giving you?

_____

_____

_____

_____

_____

_____

_____

_____

_____

_____

Take a few minutes to read again some of God's messages to you. Did He ask you any questions? Have you answered His questions and thanked Him for His loving companionship? Continue the practice of watching for God's questions in scripture, and listening in your personal quiet times as you move ahead to the emphasis of the next section: "Listening with an Obedient Spirit."

LISTENING WITH AN OBEDIENT SPIRIT

Genesis 6 shows us that listening to God and obeying Him would save humanity from the consequences of wrongdoing. It also reveals that disobedience grieves God and fills Him with pain.

The Lord saw how great man's wickedness on the earth had become, and that every inclination of the thoughts of his heart was only evil all the time. The Lord was grieved that he had made man on the earth, and his heart was filled with pain *(Genesis 6:5-6)*.

Noah, son of Lamech and grandson of the oldest man named in Genesis, Methuselah, was given a name that's associated with comfort.[1] Noah walked in close fellowship with God, and God let Noah in on His plan when He saw that the earth was filled with violence.

This is the account of Noah.

Noah was a righteous man, blameless among the people of his time, and he walked with God. Noah had three sons: Shem, Ham and Japheth.

Now the earth was corrupt in God's sight and was full of violence. God saw how corrupt the earth had become, for all the people on earth had corrupted their ways. So God said to Noah, "I am going to put an end to all people, for the earth is filled with violence because of them. I am surely going to destroy both them and the earth. So make yourself an ark of cypress wood; make rooms in it and coat it with pitch inside and out" *(Genesis 6:9-14)*.

God then proceeded to tell Noah how to build something he had never seen. As preposterous as it seemed, "Noah did everything just as God commanded him" (Genesis 6:22). Every step of the way, Noah listened to God's instructions:

"So make yourself an ark" (Genesis 6:14).

"Go into the ark" (Genesis 7:1).

"Come out of the ark" (Genesis 8:15).

God's conversations continued with Noah after the flood, and His covenant was given, promising never to destroy all living creatures on the earth by flood again. As a reminder of this covenant, God placed the rainbow in the sky.

● ● ● ● ● ●

I was 16 when God spoke to my heart and asked me to help get a church of my denomination started in my town. He may just as well have said, "Build an ark." I was on a holiday trip with my best friend and her parents to visit her aunt. Our main purpose was to attend a special New Year's revival at her aunt's church. I was along for a fun trip and was enjoying the music and excitement of the service. The evangelist giving the message was dynamic, although I don't remember one word of his sermon. The Holy Spirit was speaking to my heart, and at the close of the service, I found myself weeping at the altar. I did not hear audible words, yet in my heart God's Spirit had breathed His message, and I knew I was being given an assignment bigger than I could imagine. I shared this with my friend as she knelt beside me. Her advice was for me to talk to her father, who was my pastor, and ask him what I should do next.

As frightened and resistant as I was at the altar that night, the call was clear. Even though I didn't really know how the total picture would unfold, I obeyed and followed each step as He led me. A church still exists and is ministering in that town today. Through the years people have believed and trusted in Jesus and, in the words of Jesus to Nicodemus in John 3, have been "born again."

The first mention of the Holy Spirit in the Bible is in Genesis 1:2, in anticipation of order and wonder.[2] It interests me that the second reference to the Holy Spirit is found in Noah's story in Genesis 6:3, this time in anticipation of destruction.[3] Although the Spirit is mentioned numerous times between Genesis in the Old Testament and John in the New Testament, the conversation between Jesus and Nicodemus in John 3 is revealing. Jesus uses wind as an illustration of the point He makes about being born of the Spirit and is explaining to Nicodemus what this means.

> The wind blows wherever it pleases. You hear its sound, but you cannot tell where it comes from or where it is going. So it is with everyone born of the Spirit (*John 3:8*).

Nicodemus was confused and asked how this could be. Read this exciting passage of scripture in John 3:1-42. This is a life-changing word from Jesus to Nicodemus and to all of us today. Read John 3:16 as if you had never heard it before: "God so loved the world that He gave his one and only Son, that whoever believes in him shall not perish but have eternal life" (John 3:16).

Have you been born again? Do you have the assurance of eternal life? This is key to hearing what God wants to say to you as you wait in His presence and listen for His message to you.

The scripture does not tell us whether or not Nicodemus truly believed and was born again that night. However, it seems clear that at some point he had a trusting and believing experience, because in John 19:38-41 we read that he boldly accompanied Joseph of Arimathea to bury the body of Jesus.

• • • • • •

A pastor shared with me once that during his drinking days, when he was powerless to change, he found himself driving on the freeway with both the radio and CB at full volume. That was his escape from the reality of what was happening to his life. He said a voice from somewhere, not audible but powerfully clear, said *Turn off the radios.* He obeyed. He had never experienced anything like what happened next. The Spirit of Jesus became very real as if Jesus himself sat in the passenger seat. The pastor remembers the exact words spoken to him: *Believe in me and trust me today, and I will never leave you or forsake you.*

My friend says that he was not one to cry, but he began weeping and could hardly drive. He believed in Jesus and trusted Him that day, and Jesus has never left him nor forsaken him. His wife and other witnesses confirm his testimony that he never touched alcohol again—something he had been powerless to do in his own strength. He immediately began to tell others about Jesus, and for years now, God has used him to minister to others.

• • • • • •

Throughout biblical and contemporary history, no two stories are exactly the same. However, it's more likely that we'll hear the message of the Holy Spirit if we turn off the radio and TV and remove ourselves from the noise that drowns out His voice. I'm not declaring that you'll hear an audible voice, but what you sense the Lord saying will definitely be consistent with Scripture and the holy character of the Father, Son, and Holy Spirit.

As Jesus explained to Nicodemus, the Spirit is like the wind. You can hear the wind blowing and see evidence of its movement, but you can't tell where it came from or where it's going next. "So it is with everyone born of the Spirit" (John 3:8).

Did Noah hear an audible voice from God? I don't know. Did Nicodemus hear an audible voice? Yes, from Jesus, the Son of God. Did my friend hear an audible voice? No, but the voice of the Holy Spirit was clearly spoken to his heart.

I don't know if you'll hear an audible voice. This I do know: God will speak clearly to your heart when you read scripture prayerfully, and the more you listen and obey, the clearer His voice will become to you. If you've never been born of the Spirit as Jesus explained to Nicodemus, your first step of obedience is to believe and trust in Him.

Last month you looked at some of the questions God asked. I don't read of God asking Noah questions or Noah questioning God. However, Nicodemus had a couple of questions for Jesus:

"How can a man be born when he is old?" (John 3:4).

"How can this be?" (John 3:9).

Jesus had a question for Nicodemus: "You are Israel's teacher . . . and you do not understand these things?" (John 3:10).

Last month it was suggested that you answer the question Jesus asked the blind man: "What do you want me to do for you?" (Luke 18:41). The challenge of this month is to speak that same question to Jesus: "What do you want me to do for you?" It will not likely be to build an ark. It may not be to help start a new church; however, He will no doubt say, *Believe in me and trust me today.*

Many of the passages you'll read in this section are the words of Jesus. Listening while reading scripture is actually a form of praying. Calvin Miller says, "There's but a thin line that separates the devotional reading of and praying of Scriptures. When the heart adores Christ as it reads the Bible, it transcends the act of repeating mere words. When we read the Bible while fixed on Christ, it becomes an act of adoration. Our reading then becomes *prayer.*"[4]

Sit in adoration at the feet of Jesus, and allow Him to speak His wisdom to you.

Focus for the Month:

Genesis 5:21-9:17

John 2-4, 16-21

TODAY IS _____

Listen through scripture:

JOHN 4:39-42

Many of the Samaritans from that town believed in him because of the woman's testimony. "He told me everything I ever did." So when the Samaritans came to him, they urged him to stay with them, and he stayed two days. And because of his words many more became believers. They said to the woman, "We no longer believe just because of what you said; now we have heard for ourselves, and we know that this man really is the Savior of the world."

What I sensed God saying to me:

This is a new day. I will be with you again today. Don't miss the beauty of my world. Treat all people you meet as if they're valuable, because they truly are valuable. Practice courtesy and gentleness.

What message is God giving you?

_____

_____

_____

_____

_____

_____

_____

_____

_____

_____

_____

TODAY IS _____

Listen through scripture:

JOHN 16:7-10:

I tell you the truth: It is for your good that I am going away. Unless I go away, the Counselor will not come to you; but if I go, I will send him to you. When he comes, he will convict the world of guilt in regard to sin and righteousness and judgment: in regard to sin, because men do not believe in me; in regard to righteousness, because I am going to the Father, where you can see me no longer.

What I sensed God saying to me:

Thank you for coming to me for help with your problems. I am your source of wisdom, strength, peace, and joy. I will continue to be with you, giving you counsel. Keep praying.

What message is God giving you?

_____

_____

_____

_____

_____

_____

_____

_____

_____

_____

TODAY IS _____

Listen through scripture:

JOHN 16:13:

> *When he, the Spirit of truth, comes, he will guide you into all truth. He will not speak on his own; he will speak only what he hears, and he will tell you what is yet to come.*

What I sensed God saying to me:

> *I have created you to do good works for me this very day. Don't worry about the weather or circumstances. I will go with you wherever you go. Come to me for wisdom in all of your decisions, great or small. Then you won't have to wonder, Did I make the right choice? Never fail to keep this time apart with me.*

What message is God giving you?

_____

_____

_____

_____

_____

_____

_____

_____

_____

_____

_____

TODAY IS _____

Listen through scripture:

JOHN 17:3-5:

Now this is eternal life: that they may know you, the only true God, and Jesus Christ, whom you have sent. I have brought you glory on earth by completing the work you gave me to do. And now, Father, glorify me in your presence with the glory I had with you before the world began.

What I sensed God saying to me:

Lo, I am wiwth you to the very end. You were not created for this world of sin and chaos. I am preparing you for a better world. Give me your fears and anxieties, your doubts and worries.

What message is God giving you?

_____

_____

_____

_____

_____

_____

_____

_____

_____

_____

_____

_____

TODAY IS _____

Listen through scripture:

JOHN 17:20-23:

My prayer is not for them alone. I pray also for those who will believe in me through their message, that all of them may be one, Father, just as you are in me and I am in you. May they also be in us so that the world may believe that you have sent me. I have given them the glory that you gave me, that they may be one as we are one: I in them and you in me. May they be brought to complete unity to let the world know that you sent me and have loved them even as you have loved me.

What I sensed God saying to me:

You were created for a purpose. Look to me as you make moment-to-moment decisions as well as lifetime decisions. Every one, no matter how seemingly insignificant, is life-changing. While no person is superior to others, some individuals use their gifts and abilities to impact the world for good. Make yourself totally available to me, and be alert to ways you can make a positive impact on your world.

What message is God giving you?

_____

_____

_____

_____

_____

_____

_____

_____

_____

TODAY IS _____

Listen through scripture:

JOHN 18:36:

My kingdom is not of this world. If it were, my servants would fight to prevent my arrest by the Jews. But now my kingdom is from another place.

What I sensed God saying to me:

Surrender everything to me today. Here are some things I want you to surrender: your family, your home, your agenda today, your schedule for this week, your coming and going. Surrender the known and the unknown, the seen and the unseen, the present and the future, health and sickness, strengths and weaknesses.

What message is God giving you?

_____

_____

_____

_____

_____

_____

_____

_____

_____

_____

_____

_____

TODAY IS _____

Listen through scripture:

JOHN 19:38-39:

Later, Joseph of Arimathea asked Pilate for the body of Jesus. Now Joseph was a disciple of Jesus, but secretly because he feared the Jews. With Pilate's permission, he came and took the body away. He was accompanied by Nicodemus, the man who earlier had visited Jesus at night. Nicodemus brought a mixture of myrrh and aloes, about seventy-five pounds.

What I sensed God saying to me:

I see your tattered emotions; I hear your cry for repentance. I hear you when you say, "I'm sorry." I have been with you every day of your life. I will be with you today. I am transforming your life. I will continue to lead you and give you wisdom and understanding. I hear your cries for others. I will be here. Trust my timing in your life and theirs.

What message is God giving you?

_____

_____

_____

_____

_____

_____

_____

_____

_____

_____

TODAY IS _____

Listen through scripture:

JOHN 20:15:

> *"Woman," he said, "why are you crying? Who is it you are looking for?"*

What I sensed God saying to me:

Persevere. Keep your eyes on me, not on the problems. I will give you peace in the midst of every storm. I will give grace and glory. Life is made up of unexpected twists and turns, sorrows and joys, disappointments and gladness, surprises and routine, confusion and tough decisions. I will be with you in each and every situation today, tomorrow, next week, next month, and always.

What message is God giving you?

_____

_____

_____

_____

_____

_____

_____

_____

_____

_____

_____

_____

TODAY IS _____

Listen through scripture:

JOHN 20:19-20:

On the evening of that first day of the week, when the disciples were together, with the doors locked for fear of the Jews, Jesus came and stood among them and said, "Peace be with you!" After he said this, he showed them his hands and side. The disciples were overjoyed when they saw the Lord.

What I sensed God saying to me:

Bring joy to my world. I will give you alertness. Smile often. The world is full of heavy hearts, busy steps, scowling faces, and eyes that don't see. Slow down and enjoy each experience. Find me waiting in the unexpected places.

What message is God giving you?

_____

_____

_____

_____

_____

_____

_____

_____

_____

_____

_____

TODAY IS _____

Listen through scripture:

JOHN 20:28-29:

> *Thomas said to him, "My Lord and my God!"*
> *Then Jesus told him, "Because you have seen me, you have believed; blessed are those who have not seen and yet have believed."*

What I sensed God saying to me:

> *Believe—no matter what happens. Trust—even in the unknown. Hope in the midst of uncertainty. Love in spite of your circumstances. Give me your tiredness, your energy, your emotions, your joy, your despair, your all. Abandon yourself to me.*

What message is God giving you?

_____

_____

_____

_____

_____

_____

_____

_____

_____

_____

TODAY IS _____

Listen through scripture:

JOHN 20:30:

Jesus did many other miraculous signs in the presence of his disciples, which are not recorded in this book. But these are written that you may believe that Jesus is the Christ, the Son of God, and that by believing you may have life in his name.

What I sensed God saying to me:

Just look around you at the wonders of my world! Look for wonder in your world. You'll see it all around you. Don't miss a single detail.

What message is God giving you?

_____

_____

_____

_____

_____

_____

_____

_____

_____

_____

_____

_____

TODAY IS _____

Listen through scripture:

JOHN 21:5-6:

> He called out to them, "Friends, haven't you any fish?"
> "No," they answered.
> He said, "Throw your net on the right side of the boat and you will find some." When they did, they were unable to haul the net in because of the large number of fish.

What I sensed God saying to me:

Each day will be a new adventure with me. Live it to the fullest with joy and celebration. Cherish each day. Don't let a moment slip by unnoticed. Too many days and moments in life go by taken for granted and unnoticed by my children. There is still so much I have to teach you. As you are learning, I will use you to teach others—often when you least expect it. You've heard me say that before, haven't you?

What message is God giving you?

_____

_____

_____

_____

_____

_____

_____

_____

_____

TODAY IS _____

Listen through scripture:

JOHN 21:7:

> *Then the disciple whom Jesus loved said to Peter, "It is the Lord!"*

What I sensed God saying to me:

> *I am your Lord and Master. You are forgiven, clean, and perfect in my eyes. I adore you; I gave my life for you; I created you; and I delight in spending time with you.*

What message is God giving you?

_____

_____

_____

_____

_____

_____

_____

_____

_____

_____

_____

_____

_____

TODAY IS _____

Listen through scripture:

JOHN 21:10-12:

> Jesus said to them, "Bring some of the fish you have just caught."
>
> Simon Peter climbed aboard and dragged the net ashore. It was full of large fish, 153, but even with so many the net was not torn. Jesus said to them, "Come and have breakfast." None of the disciples dared ask him, "Who are you?" They knew it was the Lord.

What I sensed God saying to me:

> Take nothing for granted. I will give you wisdom. Although you are not perfect and make mistakes, I will use your mistakes as learning experiences in your life. You are aware that I don't always reveal everything to you. I save some things for wonder and surprises. I will reveal only what you need to know for the work I ask you to do. But with each task I ask you to do, you'll be given insight, and I'll give you a fresh anointing and power to perform it.

What message is God giving you?

_____

_____

_____

_____

_____

_____

_____

_____

_____

_____

TODAY IS _____

Listen through scripture:

JOHN 21:25:

Jesus did many other things as well. If every one of them were written down, I suppose that even the whole world would not have room for the books that would be written.

What I sensed God saying to me:

Life is fragile; treat it tenderly, both your own life and the lives of others. Life is fleeting; accept each moment as a gift. Life is an adventure; live it to the fullest. Life has a purpose; fulfill the tasks I give you to do. Life is holy; live it with me. Take me with you wherever you go. Don't leave me out of one activity. Spectator worship is not for you. Worship me today. Weep with me over a lost world. Rejoice with me over victories.

What message is God giving you?

_____

_____

_____

_____

_____

_____

_____

_____

_____

_____

_____

Richard Ortberg says, "Every time someone says yes to God, the world changes a little bit."[5] On the other hand, Ortberg says, "Every time you say no to God—you change a little. Your heart gets a little harder. Your spirit dies a little. Your addiction to comfort gets a little stronger."[6] Those are powerful thoughts for personal reflection.

LISTENING TO CONVERSATIONS

God doesn't just ask us questions, probe for answers, ask us to listen for His instruction and then obey. He allows us to ask Him questions. This month we'll explore conversations between God and Abraham (Abram) and note some of the bold questions Abraham asked God.

The Lord asked Abram to leave his country and go to the land to which God would lead him. Abram obeyed and set out for Canaan, taking his wife and nephew along as well as his servants and possessions. (See Genesis 12:1-5.)

Along the way, Abram built altars and called on the name of the Lord. When Abram came to Canaan, the Lord promised this land to his offspring, and he built an altar. (See Genesis 12:7-8.)

God spoke to Abram after he and Lot separated their livestock, and again Abram built an altar to the Lord. (See Genesis 13:18.)

In Genesis 15 the Lord spoke to Abram in a vision and said, "Do not be afraid, Abram, for I will protect you, and your reward will be great" (v. 1, NLT). Abram began to ask God some bold questions.

"But Abram replied, 'O Sovereign Lord, what good are all your blessings when I don't even have a son?'" (v. 2).

The dialogue continued with God asking Abram to count the stars in the sky and promising him that many descendants (v. 5).

The conversation was then interrupted by the famous faith verse: "And Abram believed the Lord, and the Lord counted him as righteous because of his faith (v. 6, NLT).

"Then the Lord told him, 'I am the Lord who brought you out of Ur of the Chaldeans to give you this land as your possession'" (v. 7, NLT).

Instead of thanking the Lord, Abram had the courage to say, "O Sovereign Lord, how can I be sure that I will actually possess it?" (v. 8, NLT).

God didn't seem at all upset with Abram because of his questions. He responded by sealing the covenant in an act that Abram would understand as binding in his culture. In chapter 17 Abram's name was changed to Abraham.

Chapter 18 is filled with questions both by the Lord and Abraham.

When my husband, Curtis, and I were called to minister in a state we had never even visited, I felt a little as I imagine Abraham felt when God called him to leave his family and travel to a land where He would lead him. We experienced excitement as well as uncertainty. Curtis and I had agreed that when he graduated from seminary we would go to a place only when we were absolutely sure God was saying yes. That place turned out to be New Jersey. Curtis was a Kentucky boy, and I had spent all my school years through college in Tennessee. Neither of us had ever been to New Jersey, and neither of us knew anyone living in New Jersey. We had not seen the church or the parsonage, and we had not met anyone who attended the church.

Our next move was to a town I had never visited and a church, parsonage, and group of people I had never seen. We had been at that assignment about two years when another church invited my husband to interview. After initially declining, he finally agreed as a courtesy to the leader who called him and the board extending the invitation. As Curtis left home to travel to the interview, he said he didn't know why he had agreed to go. I wasn't sure if he felt that way because he thought he was wasting his time and theirs or because of the problems we knew the church was facing.

That night after our two young children were in bed, I prayed and told God not to let Curtis allow that church board to talk him into anything. God promptly asked me, *What if I want him to go?*

That's when I began questioning God. *What about the fact that we've been here only two years? That doesn't seem long enough. We're just beginning to see progress and growth in this declining congregation.*

God's response was *Who's to say how long is long enough?*

But, God, what will the people think? They won't understand; they've been very good to us here.

God's said, *Let me handle that.*

But, God, what about my neighbors? Two neighbor ladies were in my new believers' Bible study.

God said, *Don't you think I can take care of my children?*

What about my babies? Our church nursery supervisor lived across the street from us and was our babysitter.

For every question, God had a rapid response. I didn't know if we were leaving or if God was testing me. In a few short weeks we were moving. Our congregation was gracious, and God gave me a plan for finding someone else to lead the new believers' Bible study. He sent one of my best friends to live in the parsonage I was leaving. She and her husband became close friends with my neighbor and helped disciple her. The nursery supervisor moved, and God took care of my children at our new location.

There have been many moves since, and God has revealed His plan in a different way each time. Although the circumstances are not the same, we made decisions based on prayer and confirmation through scripture, church leaders, other believers, and open doors. It seems that Abraham's only source was his conversations with God.

We have a high and holy privilege today through the work of the Holy Spirit and Scripture to hear from the Savior of the world and to dialogue with Him as we give Him our questions and listen for His responses.

Any deep conversations between two people involve both speaking and listening. Focus on listening to your conversations this month.

Listen to what you're telling yourself. Is your self-talk telling your mind the truth? William Backus and Marie Chapian in their book *Telling Yourself the Truth* say that many people have what are called "misbeliefs" that they continually tell themselves that cause them to form an inaccurate belief system. The book gives scripturally based beliefs to counter misbeliefs.[1]

Listen to the questions you ask yourself and to your own responses. Weigh these questions and responses against scripture, and make conscious changes if you're deceiving yourself.

Don't forget to listen to your conversations with others. Is there a shred of deception there to protect yourself as Abraham did in the last part of Genesis 12 when He took his clan into Egypt during the famine and again with King Abimelech in chapter 15? Confess, and—like Abraham—pray to God.

In order to hold to His Word and know truth, you must be into His Word, reading it, studying it, listening carefully.

As you study the life of Abraham this month, I suggest that you use *The Narrated Bible in Chronological Order* with devotional commentary by F. LaGard Smith. Concise, abbreviated historical accounts and explanations of the significance of events are inserted between passages of Scripture. These summaries give great insight into the relationship between God and Abraham.[2]

As you read scripture, stop every few verses and ask God what He's saying to you personally from this passage. Give Him time to respond before reading more. In this way you can be in conversation with your Creator as you read the Bible. Also, turn scripture into prayer. Calvin Miller says this is the best way to develop the art of listening prayer. "We too often go into God's presence with a list of pleas, trying to talk God into granting our desires. But this kind of praying makes us 'one big mouth' and God 'one grand ear.' But when we pray the Scriptures, it makes God the voice and leaves us as the ear. In short, God gets his turn at getting a word in edgewise."[3]

Pour out your heart to God; ask Him questions. After each question, pause for Him to answer. He may not give you an immediate answer, but at least you've given Him the opportunity if He's ready to reveal it to you. Watch and listen intently throughout the day; the answer may come at an unexpected time and place. Even if He delays, as He did in keeping His promise of a son to Abraham, believe that He has heard your prayer and is working.

Focus for the Month:

Genesis 11-25
John 4
Hebrews 7; 11:8-19

TODAY IS _____

Listen through scripture:

GENESIS 12:1, 3, NLT:

The LORD had said to Abram, "Leave your native country, your relatives, and your father's family and go to the land that I will show you. . . . All the families on earth will be blessed through you."

What I sensed God saying to me:

Go into the world where I send you. Give an abundance of love and blessings. Never be proud or pious. Be transparent, caring, courteous, and kind.

What message is God giving you?

_____

_____

_____

_____

_____

_____

_____

_____

_____

_____

_____

_____

TODAY IS _____

Listen through scripture:

GENESIS 12:4:

So Abram left, as the LORD had told him; and Lot went with him. Abram was seventy-five years old when he set out from Haran.

What I sensed God saying to me:

Life is full of many puzzles and hardships. There's no escaping them on earth. No place will feel like home, nor will you lead a life without hurts, until you get to heaven. Don't look for the perfect place or expect it.

What message is God giving you?

_____

_____

_____

_____

_____

_____

_____

_____

_____

_____

_____

_____

_____

_____

_____

TODAY IS _____

Read Genesis 12:8 and Genesis 13:1-4

Listen through scripture:

GENESIS 12:8, NLT:

After that, Abram traveled south and set up camp in the hill country, with Bethel to the west and Ai to the east. There he built another altar and dedicated it to the LORD, and he worshiped the LORD.

What I sensed God saying to me:

Keep listening to my voice. Don't neglect these times with me. Never use these thoughts for the wrong reasons or motives. I have received your prayer of surrender and accepted your self-sacrifice of your surrender of your will and your recommitment of your life and future to me. I know there's a struggle between the temporal and spiritual, between the ways of the world and my ways. Call on me in every situation.

What message is God giving you?

_____

_____

_____

_____

_____

_____

_____

_____

_____

TODAY IS _____

Read Genesis 14:1-20

Listen through scripture:

GENESIS 14:18-20, NLT:

Melchizedek, the King of Salem and a priest of God Most High, brought Abram some bread and wine. Melchizedek blessed Abram with this blessing: "Blessed be Abram by God Most High, Creator of heaven and earth. And blessed be God Most High, who has defeated your enemies for you."

What I sensed God saying to me:

My love overflows to you. You don't have to earn it or even measure up to receive it. It's not necessary to be productive every moment of the day. Rest is important.

What message is God giving you?

_____

_____

_____

_____

_____

_____

_____

_____

_____

_____

_____

TODAY IS _____

Listen through scripture:

GENESIS 15:1, NLT:

Some time later, the LORD spoke to Abram in a vision and said to him, "Do not be afraid, Abram, for I will protect you, and your reward will be great."

What I sensed God saying to me:

Display love to all people you meet, including those of your own household. Give me your past, present, and future. I know the plans I have for you. Don't try to figure them all out. Don't fear, for I'm with you, protecting and guiding, strengthening and helping.

What message is God giving you?

_____

_____

_____

_____

_____

_____

_____

_____

_____

_____

_____

_____

_____

TODAY IS _____

Read Genesis 16

Listen through scripture:

GENESIS 16:13:

She [Hagar] gave this name to the LORD who spoke to her: "You are the God who sees me," for she said, "I have now seen the One who sees me."

What I sensed God saying to me:

Yes, I see even your moments of desperation and weakness. Let go of imperfections quickly, and move on. Feeling remorseful for a moment is fine as you make a plan not to repeat the same mistakes, but don't let past errors immobilize you. Allow me to show you things in your heart and voice that could be labeled as complaining.

What message is God giving you?

_____

_____

_____

_____

_____

_____

_____

_____

_____

_____

TODAY IS _____

Read Genesis 18:16-21

GENESIS 18:17-19:

> Then the LORD said, "Shall I hide from Abraham what I am about to do?
> Abraham will surely become a great and powerful nation, and all nations on
> earth will be blessed through him. For I have chosen him, so that he will direct
> his children and his household after him to keep the way of the LORD by doing
> what is right and just, so that the LORD will bring about for Abraham what he
> has promised him.

What I sensed God saying to me:

> I will work through you today. Life is made up of moments. Cherish each
> one, even those that seem to be bad. Can you look back and see how I have
> taken bad and used it for good? I know my ways are hard for you to compre-
> hend.

What message is God giving you?

_____

_____

_____

_____

_____

_____

_____

_____

_____

_____

_____

TODAY IS _____

Read Genesis 19:1-19 and 2 Peter 2:4-9

Listen through scripture:

GENESIS 19:27-28:

Early the next morning Abraham got up and returned to the place where he had stood before the LORD. He looked down toward Sodom and Gomorrah, toward all the land of the plain, and he saw dense smoke rising from the land, like smoke from a furnace.

What I sensed God saying to me:

Return to the place where you last met me. Gaze intently around you and tell me what you see. What do you believe I see?

What message is God giving you?

_____

_____

_____

_____

_____

_____

_____

_____

_____

_____

_____

_____

TODAY IS _____

Listen through scripture:

GENESIS 21:33:

Abraham planted a tamarisk tree in Beersheba, and there he called upon the name of the LORD, the Eternal God.

What I sensed God saying to me:

I am the Eternal God. You're discovering the truth that there's no paradise on earth; there will be no perfect life here. Expect it and accept it. Don't forget—I'll lead you one step at a time, and I'll direct your future.

What message is God giving you?

_____

_____

_____

_____

_____

_____

_____

_____

_____

_____

_____

_____

_____

_____

TODAY IS _____

Listen through scripture:

GENESIS 25:7-8, NLT:

Abraham lived for 175 years, and he died at a ripe old age, having lived a long and satisfying life. He breathed his last and joined his ancestors in death.

What I sensed God saying to me:

Leave a legacy for future generations. Live only to please me and me alone.

What message is God giving you?

_____

_____

_____

_____

_____

_____

_____

_____

_____

_____

_____

_____

_____

_____

TODAY IS _____

Listen through scripture:

ROMANS 4:1-5, NLT:

Abraham was, humanly speaking, the founder of our Jewish nation. What did he discover about being made right with God? If his good deeds had made him acceptable to God, he would have had something to boast about. But that was not God's way. For the Scriptures tell us, "Abraham believed God, and God counted him as righteous because of his faith." When people work, their wages are not a gift, but something they have earned. But people are counted as righteous, not because of their work, but because of their faith in God who forgives sinners.

What I sensed God saying to me:

Don't try to impress others with your conversations. Don't try to find favor from others by your actions. Check every thought and motive, and bring each one under my subjection. Keep a smile in your heart. Don't ever think of yourself as a better Christian than others. Accept my love and the love of others graciously.

What message is God giving you?

_____

_____

_____

_____

_____

_____

_____

_____

TODAY IS _____

Listen through scripture:

HEBREWS 5:7-10, NLT:

While Jesus was here on earth, he offered prayers and pleadings, with a loud cry and tears, to the one who could rescue him from death. And God heard his prayers because of his deep reverence for God. Even though Jesus was God's Son, he learned obedience from the things he suffered. In this way, God qualified him as a perfect High Priest, and he became the source of eternal salvation for all those who obey him. And God designated him to be a High Priest in the order of Melchizedek.

What I sensed God saying to me:

You have discovered through the years that intercessory prayer is hard work. Don't operate by your feelings alone, although they're an indicator to you. Remember that I am interceding to the Father for you. Make the end of the day more relaxing. This will be to your advantage.

What message is God giving you?

_____

_____

_____

_____

_____

_____

_____

_____

_____

_____

TODAY IS _____

Listen through scripture:

HEBREWS 6:16-18, NLT:

Now when people take an oath, they call on someone greater than themselves to hold them to it. And without any question that oath is binding. God also bound himself with an oath, so that those who received the promise could be perfectly sure that he would never change his mind. So God has given both his promise and his oath. These two things are unchangeable because it is impossible for God to lie. Therefore, we who have fled to him for refuge can have great confidence as we hold to the hope that lies before us.

What I sensed God saying to me:

My words are true. Your hope is in me. I have called you. You are mine.

What message is God giving you?

_____

_____

_____

_____

_____

_____

_____

_____

_____

_____

_____

_____

TODAY IS _____

Listen through scripture:

HEBREWS 7:24-26, NLT:

Because Jesus lives forever, his priesthood lasts forever. Therefore he is able, once and forever, to save those who come to God through him. He lives forever to intercede with God on their behalf. He is the kind of high priest we need because he is holy and blameless, unstained by sin. He has been set apart from sinners and has been given the highest place of honor in heaven.

What I sensed God saying to me:

I have you here for a purpose. I will move you when that purpose is fulfilled or when I have a new job for you to do. Don't get sidetracked. Keep your eyes on only me, not on the temporal.

What message is God giving you?

_____

_____

_____

_____

_____

_____

_____

_____

_____

_____

_____

_____

LISTENING BEYOND REQUESTS

From Genesis 11 to the end of the book, we are focused on Abraham, a man of incredible faith, and his descendants. LaGard Smith says, "In the years covered by the Genesis record, the outstanding man of God was Abraham. It was Abraham who fathered the nation which would become God's chosen people. It was Abraham whose belief and trust in God's promises made him an example of faith for all times."[1]

The last half of the book of Genesis gives stories from the life of Abraham's promised son, Isaac, and Isaac's son, Jacob, whose name God later changed to Israel. The book of Genesis ends with the death of Joseph, Israel's beloved son, and years pass before we find another scriptural account of the Israelites.

Exodus, the second book of the Bible, centers around Moses, the man God chose to lead the Hebrew nation out of Egyptian slavery and the bondage they fell into after the death of Joseph. "As the Exodus record begins, a new spiritual leader emerges from among God's people. For a more sophisticated age, Moses will be a man of education, training, and royal upbringing. He will be an author, lawgiver, builder, and military leader. Most importantly, he, like Abraham, will be a man of faith in God and an intermediary between God and his people."[2]

Exodus opens with a record of the sons of Israel who went into Egypt and how they multiplied and were oppressed when the new king, who did not know Joseph, came into power. (See Exodus 1:1-14.)

To control the population growth of the Israelites, the king, known as Pharaoh, ordered the baby boys to be killed. A well-loved Bible story tells about the midwives refusing the king's orders and how baby Moses was hidden by his mother in a basket among the reeds along the bank of the Nile. Moses was discovered by Pharaoh's daughter, and a series of events resulted in Moses eventually being raised in the palace. (See Exodus 2.)

God speaks in a variety of ways in both ordinary and unusual circumstances, when we least expect it, and when we wait expectantly. However, only one time in Scripture does God speak from a burning bush. The first time God spoke to Moses was when Moses was tending his flocks. Before the dramatic burning bush account of God calling Moses to be the deliverer of His children in Exodus 3, a key scripture is given:

> The Israelites groaned in their slavery and cried out, and their cry for help because of their slavery went up to God. God heard their groaning and he remembered his covenant with Abraham, with Isaac and with Jacob. So God looked on the Israelites and was concerned about them *(Exodus 2:23-25).*

Moses and God carried on a lively conversation beside the bush, and in Exodus 4:13 Moses begged God to send someone else to do the task God was giving him. God didn't answer the request in the way Moses expected. He didn't release Moses from the task but agreed to send Aaron, who was more fluent in speech, to go with Moses to be his spokesperson.

We find Moses arguing and pleading with God throughout Exodus:

> Then Moses went back to the LORD and protested, "Why have you brought all this trouble on your own people, Lord? Why did you send me? Ever since I came to Pharaoh as your spokesman, he has been even more brutal to y*our people.* And you have done nothing to rescue them! *(Exodus 5:22-23, NLT).*

God reassured Moses with these words:

> Then the LORD told Moses, "Now you will see what I will do to Pharaoh. When he feels the force of my strong hand, he will let the people go. In fact, he will force them to leave his land!"

> And God said to Moses, "I am Yahweh—'the LORD.' I appeared to Abraham, to Isaac, and to Jacob as El-Shaddai—'God Almighty'—but I did not reveal my name, Yahweh, to them. And I reaffirmed my covenant with them. Under its terms, I promised to give them the land of Canaan, where they were living as foreigners. You can be sure that I have heard the groans of the people of Israel, who are now slaves to the Egyptians. And I am well aware of my covenant with them" *(Exodus 6:1-5, NLT).*

Have you ever obeyed God and found circumstances getting worse?

From Exodus through Deuteronomy we find Moses making requests, crying, interceding for his people, and pleading for them. He argued with God and begged Him to show His glory. Answers came in unpredictable ways.

• • • • • •

In his late 20s, Jim Cymbala, pastor of Brooklyn Tabernacle in New York City, received an answer from God while he was on a fishing boat in

Florida recovering from a hacking cough and dealing with despair over his inadequacies and the needs of his church. "Then quietly but forcefully, in words heard not in my ear but deep within my spirit, I sensed God speaking."[3]

The advice he heard was to lead his people to pray, and he would always have something fresh to preach, enough finances, and overflowing crowds. "I knew I had heard from God, even though I had not experienced some strange vision, nothing sensational or peculiar. God was simply focusing on the only answer to our situation—or anybody else's, for that matter."[4]

That was a dynamic turning point for Jim Cymbala and his ministry. "As the boat docked later that afternoon, I felt wonderfully calm. . . . God had promised to provide, to respond to our cries for divine help. We were not alone, attempting the impossible in a heartless world. God was present, and he would act on our behalf."[5]

God's miracles continue at Brooklyn Tabernacle as Jim and Carol Cymbala obey and lead their people to make prayer a priority.

• • • • • •

In Luke 10 Martha also got an unexpected answer from Jesus when she complained to Him about her sister, Mary, who was sitting at His feet listening to His teaching while Martha did all the work.

"Lord, doesn't it seem unfair to you that my sister just sits here while I do all the work? Tell her to come and help me."

But the Lord said to her, "My dear Martha, you are worried and upset over all these details! There is only one thing worth being concerned about. Mary has discovered it, and it will not be taken away from her" *(Luke 10: 40-42, NLT).*

• • • • • •

Is God stretching you out of your comfort zone by giving you a responsibility that causes you to protest like Moses and Pastor Cymbala? Perhaps, as in His response to Martha, He's telling you to say no to some good things in order to spend time with Him.

Are you feeling inadequate as Moses and Jim Cymbala did? Are you overwhelmed by the needs and task God has set before you? Do you feel burned out as Martha felt? Are you hungering for a breakthrough of God's Spirit? Are you tired of living a powerless Christian life? Are you longing for your life to count?

If you answered yes to any of these questions, here are some things you can do:

- Call on the name of the Lord. Read Genesis 4:25-26. That is where every personal revival and movement of God among His people begins.
- Lay your situation before Him as the Israelites (Exodus 2:23-25) and Jim Cymbala did.[6]
- Follow Mary's example and sit at His feet. (See Luke 10:38-42.)
- Make sure He has called you to the assignments you have accepted, then go forward, refreshed and in the power of the great I Am!

In spite of his monumental assignment, Moses found time to meet with the Lord and get instructions from Him. In the "Listen Through Scripture" section this month you'll find lessons from Moses' life and see how God used him dramatically, in spite of his weaknesses and insecurities. You'll see how Moses learned to delegate and share the load.

Jan Johnson says, "Our job then, is to pay attention to the various avenues through which God might speak. Elizabeth Barrett Browning pointed this out: 'Earth's crammed with heaven and every common bush afire with God, but only he who sees takes off his shoes. The rest sit around and pluck blackberries.' How often I've plucked blackberries, complaining about circumstances and people when my job was to take off my shoes, gaze at the fiery bush, and interact with God there."[7]

What do you do when He delays or it seems He is not responding to your pleas?

- Keep praying. Speak your prayers, write them, sing them.
- Thank Him for listening to every prayer and for working in ways you cannot see.
- Keep rejoicing and thanking Him for past answers.
- Invite others to join you in prayer.
- Pray scripture.
- Never quit!

Keep praying beyond your requests, and, as Moses did, simply ask Him to show you His glory!

Focus for the Month:

Exodus 1-7; 11-18
Luke 10
Hebrews 11:23-29

TODAY IS _____

Listen through scripture:

EXODUS 3:1-6:

Now Moses was tending the flock of Jethro his father-in-law, the priest of Midian, and he led the flock to the far side of the desert and came to Horeb, the mountain of God. There the angel of the LORD appeared to him in flames of fire from within a bush. Moses saw that though the bush was on fire it did not burn up. So Moses thought, "I will go over and see this strange sight—why the bush does not burn up."

When the LORD saw that he had gone over to look, God called to him from within the bush, "Moses! Moses!"

And Moses said, "Here I am."

"Do not come any closer," God said. "Take off your sandals, for the place where you are standing is holy ground." Then he said, "I am the God of your father, the God of Abraham, the God of Isaac and the God of Jacob." At this, Moses hid his face, because he was afraid to look at God.

What I sensed God saying to me:

Today will be a divine adventure with me. I will give you energy to accomplish the tasks I set before you. Remember: nothing is too hard for me.

What message is God giving you?

_____

_____

_____

_____

_____

_____

_____

_____

TODAY IS _____

Listen through scripture:

EXODUS 3:7-9:

The LORD said, "I have indeed seen the misery of my people in Egypt. I have heard them crying out because of their slave drivers, and I am concerned about their suffering. So I have come down to rescue them from the hand of the Egyptians and to bring them up out of that land into a good and spacious land, a land flowing with milk and honey."

What I sensed God saying to me:

There are times you are overwhelmed with the many needs and people who come to your mind in prayer or who are on your lists. I hear each name and see them where they are no matter how feeble or brief your thoughts, words, and prayers may be. Go today to be my messenger. Even friends who have walked years in my service need a human touch to remind them of my divine love for them. I will anoint you with wisdom and understanding. I will tell you when to speak and what and when to be silent and to listen and pray.

What message is God giving you?

_____

_____

_____

_____

_____

_____

_____

_____

_____

TODAY IS _____

Listen through scripture:

EXODUS 5:22-6:1, NLT:

Then Moses went back to the LORD and protested, "Why have you brought all this trouble on your own people, LORD? Why did you send me? Ever since I came to Pharaoh as your spokesman, he has been even more brutal to your people. And you have done nothing to rescue them!"

Then the LORD told Moses, "Now you will see what I will do to Pharaoh. When he feels the force of my strong hand, he will let the people go. In fact, he will force them to leave this land!"

What I sensed God saying to me:

Even when the task I have given you seems insurmountable, remember that my strong hand will be with you.

What message is God giving you?

_____

_____

_____

_____

_____

_____

_____

_____

_____

_____

_____

TODAY IS _____

Listen through scripture:

EXODUS 14:15-18:

*Then the L*ORD *said to Moses, "Why are you crying out to me? Tell the Israelites to move on. Raise your staff and stretch out your hand over the sea to divide the water so that the Israelites can go through the sea on dry ground. I will harden the hearts of the Egyptians so that they will go in after them. And I will gain glory through Pharaoh and all his army, through his chariots and his horsemen. The Egyptians will know that I am the L*ORD *when I gain glory through Pharaoh, his chariots and his horsemen."*

What I sensed God saying to me:

Wait on me for answers. Don't rush in until you have clearance from me. Don't speak in haste. Do more listening than talking. Take me into your world. Hold your head high with joy in your heart. Be alert. The enemy forces are at work. Press on, remembering that even though I am invisible, I am with you.

What message is God giving you?

_____

_____

_____

_____

_____

_____

_____

_____

_____

TODAY IS _____

Listen through scripture:

EXODUS 14:21:

Then Moses stretched out his hand over the sea, and all that night the LORD drove the sea back with a strong east wind and turned it into dry land. The waters were divided, and the Israelites went through the sea on dry ground, with a wall of water on their right and on their left.

What I sensed God saying to me:

You are here by my appointment, in my keeping, under my training, for my time. Every moment is sacred; every activity is sacred. Remember—it's okay to have fun and enjoy life. Sometimes my biblical stories make you smile, don't they? Can you get a mental picture of this one?

What message is God giving you?

_____

_____

_____

_____

_____

_____

_____

_____

_____

_____

_____

TODO IS _____

Listen through scripture:

EXODUS 14:23-25:

The Egyptians pursued them, and all Pharaoh's horses and chariots and horsemen followed them into the sea. During the last watch of the night the Lord looked down from the pillar of fire and cloud at the Egyptian army and threw it into confusion. He made the wheels of their chariots come off so that they had difficulty driving. And the Egyptians said, "Let's get away from the Israelites! The Lord is fighting for them against Egypt."

What I sensed God saying to me:

Live out your faith gently. There are many ways my children live in bondage. Be aware that you can't fix every problem or correct every error you've made in your past. Also, realize that you can't phrase every thought perfectly or respond in every situation as others need you to or expect you to respond. Free yourself from that bondage. Allow me to flow through you as I live in you. Release yourself from unreal expectations and false guilt.

What message is God giving you?

_____

_____

_____

_____

_____

_____

_____

_____

_____

_____

TODAY IS _____

Listen through scripture:

EXODUS 14:31:

When the Israelites saw the great power the LORD displayed against the Egyptians, the people feared the LORD and put their trust in him and in Moses his servant.

What I sensed God saying to me:

Capture the moment. You have done a task for me; now leave it in my keeping. Take absolutely no credit. Give all the glory to me, and you will avoid both pride and thoughts of defeat or regret. Leave all the results to me. I will continue my work for eternity.

What message is God giving you?

_____

_____

_____

_____

_____

_____

_____

_____

_____

_____

_____

TODAY IS _____

Listen through scripture:

EXODUS 15:11:

> *Who among the gods is like you, O LORD?*
> *Who is like you—*
> *majestic in holiness.*
> *awesome in glory,*
> *working wonders?*

What I sensed God saying to me:

This will be a unique day like no other. Spend the day with me, obedient to every call I give to you. Some things I ask you to do may surprise you, but you'll know clearly if the thought is from me. Share from your heart to others.

What message is God giving you?

_____

_____

_____

_____

_____

_____

_____

_____

_____

_____

_____

_____

TODAY IS _____

Listen through scripture:

EXODUS 15:18:

> The LORD will reign for ever and ever.

What I sensed God saying to me:

> Give thanks. Sit in my presence with a glad heart. Pass on the truths I reveal to you. Keep your heart open to new truths. Hold lightly to the plans you have made as you allow me to alter them or even remove them from your life. Always be ready to move in a new or different direction at my bidding.

What message is God giving you?

_____

_____

_____

_____

_____

_____

_____

_____

_____

_____

_____

_____

_____

_____

TODAY IS _____

Read Exodus 17

Listen through scripture:

EXODUS 17:15:

Moses built an altar and called it The LORD is my Banner.

What I sensed God saying to me:

Prayer is the key—use it. Keep asking the questions: Why are we doing this? What is the purpose? Is this God's plan? What is His plan?

What message is God giving you?

_____

_____

_____

_____

_____

_____

_____

_____

_____

_____

_____

_____

_____

TODAY IS _____

Listen through scripture:

EXODUS 18:19-23:

"Listen now to me and I will give you some advice, and may God be with you. You must be the people's representative before God and bring their disputes to him. Teach them the decrees and laws, and show them the way to live and the duties they are to perform. But select capable men from all the people—men who fear God, trustworthy men who hate dishonest gain—and appoint them as officials over thousands, hundreds, fifties and tens. Have them serve as judges for the people at all times, but have them bring every difficult case to you; the simple cases they can decide themselves. That will make your load lighter, because they will share it with you. If you do this and God so commands, you will be able to stand the strain, and all these people will go home satisfied."

Moses listened to his father-in-law and did everything he said.

What I sensed God saying to me:

Sometimes I speak to you through other wise individuals. Evaluate the advice of others to see if it might be coming from me.

What message is God giving you?

_____

_____

_____

_____

_____

_____

_____

_____

TODAY IS _____

Listen through scripture:

LUKE 10:25-28, NLT:

One day an expert in religious law stood up to test Jesus by asking him this question: "Teacher, what should I do to inherit eternal life?"

Jesus replied, "What does the law of Moses say? How do you read it?"

The man answered, "'You must love the LORD your God with all your heart, all your soul, all your strength, and all your mind.' And 'Love your neighbor as yourself.'"

"Right!" Jesus told him. "Do this and you will live!"

What I sensed God saying to me:

The answers are on the way. Patiently wait. Turn your thoughts to the task at hand. I am here. Acknowledge my presence. Breathe in my holiness and purity as I cleanse anew your heart and mind.

What message is God giving you?

_____

_____

_____

_____

_____

_____

_____

_____

_____

_____

_____

TODAY IS _____

Listen through scripture:

LUKE 10:41-42:

"Martha, Martha," the Lord answered, "you are worried and upset about many things, but only one thing is needed. Mary has chosen what is better, and it will not be taken away from her."

What I sensed God saying to me:

Give me first place in your events, words, thoughts, time, money, and heart.

What message is God giving you?

_____

_____

_____

_____

_____

_____

_____

_____

_____

_____

_____

_____

_____

TODAY IS _____

Listen through scripture:

HEBREWS 11:27-29, NLT:

It was by faith that Moses left the land of Egypt, not fearing the king's anger. He kept right on going because he kept his eyes on the one who is invisible. It was by faith that Moses commanded the people of Israel to keep the Passover and to sprinkle blood on the doorposts so that the angel of death would not kill their firstborn sons.

It was by faith that the people of Israel went right through the Red Sea as though they were on dry ground. But when the Egyptians tried to follow, they were all drowned.

What I sensed God saying to me:

Many of my children block my work by selfish ambitions and striking off in their own direction with their own plans, expecting me to bless what they have not first sought my guidance in doing. When a channel is blocked, I must then find another source, another person, another church.

What message is God giving you?

_____

_____

_____

_____

_____

_____

_____

_____

_____

_____

TODAY IS _____

Listen through scripture:

HEBREWS 11:1, NLT:

Faith is the confidence that what we hope for will actually happen; it gives us assurance about things we cannot see.

What I sensed God saying to me:

I am already joyfully preparing the answer to your requests. Rest in that confidence. Do not allow yourself to become bitter about any set of circumstances. Look for the good, pray prayers of blessing, and move on. Keep praying. Keep believing. Keep rejoicing in answers to come.

What message is God giving you?

_____

_____

_____

_____

_____

_____

_____

_____

_____

_____

_____

_____

_____

From Exodus through Deuteronomy we read how Moses continued to lead the complaining mass of Israelites. His many adventures included receiving the Ten Commandments on Mt. Sinai and seeing the hand of God work in unbelievable ways. He encountered heartbreak and years of wandering as he often spoke with God regarding the sins of the people and waited for His direction. Moses and God had a unique relationship in which Moses respected God but spoke very frankly with Him as with a trusted friend. God still calls leaders today and speaks to listening, honest hearts.

LISTENING WITH AN HONEST HEART

God communicates with us when we're completely up-front and transparent with Him. There isn't a more brutally honest prayer in Scripture than Moses' prayer in Numbers 11:

> Moses heard all the families standing in the doorways of their tents whining, and the LORD became extremely angry. Moses was also very aggravated. And Moses said to the LORD, "Why are you treating me, your servant, so harshly? Have mercy on me! What did I do to deserve the burden of all these people? Did I give birth to them? Did I bring them into the world? Why did you tell me to carry them in my arms like a mother carries a nursing baby? How can I carry them to the land you swore to give their ancestors? Where am I supposed to get meat for all these people? They keep whining to me, saying, 'Give us meat to eat!' I can't carry all these people by myself! The load is far too heavy! If this is how you intend to treat me, just go ahead and kill me. Do me a favor and spare me this misery!" *(vv. 10-15, NLT).*

Notice that God did not reprimand Moses, pull his credentials, fire him, or defend himself. He calmly gave him a plan of action:

> Then the LORD said to Moses, "Gather before me seventy men who are recognized as elders and leaders of Israel. Bring them to the Tabernacle to stand there with you. I will come down and talk to you there. I will take some of the Spirit that is upon you, and I will put the Spirit upon them also. They will bear the burden of the people along with you, so you will not have to carry it alone" *(vv. 16-17, NLT).*

As you continue reading the chapter, you see that God gives further instructions to Moses. Even after this wise and compassionate response, Moses continues to banter with God. Amazingly, God doesn't turn His back on Moses but replies, "Has my arm lost its power? Now you will see whether or not my word comes true!" (v. 23, NLT).

• • • • • •

My uncle lost his thriving business because of a trusted chief financial officer who kept a duplicate set of books and showed my uncle only the fraudulent ones. In a state of deep depression because of the deception and loss, my uncle cried out to God in his pain, "I cannot forgive him for what he did to me!"

He said that God spoke to his spirit immediately in one short sentence that could not have been clearer had he heard it audibly. God said, *He didn't do it to you.*

My uncle's response was, "What do you mean—he didn't do it to me? I lost everything! My business is gone! I have nothing left to start over with!"

It was then that God reminded my uncle of the night he and his son knelt at the altar of the church before starting the business and committed it to God, saying, "This business will be yours, God, totally yours."

At that point my uncle began to laugh. Knowing how my uncle was despairing, when my aunt heard his laughter she went running into the room. He told her what God had said, and she suggested they go to the kitchen, make a pot of coffee, and call their three children. They sat together at the table, drank coffee, talked, and laughed. When my aunt called the children to come over, she said, "We have your father back!"

That one message from God in response to an honest cry was a turning point that freed my uncle to move into the next chapter God had for him.

• • • • • •

What does God do when we come to Him groaning, complaining, ranting, and raving? He simply listens. Then, when we're finished, He gives sound advice.

I met Dorothy at a conference where I was speaking. After she retired from military service and a position as a bookkeeper, circumstances led her to move into a tiny box-like trailer that reminded her of one of many foster homes she had lived in as a child. She told me she had angrily approached God, pounding at His door, asking, *Why?* and begging Him to do something.

When she was exhausted and quiet, He said, "I brought you here to deal with your childhood." Although she thought she had recovered from her past, God was taking her to a deeper level of wholeness, and today she's experiencing joy and peace in her humble surroundings. She's finding Jesus, the healer of brokenness, to be enough.

●   ●   ●   ●   ●   ●

Do you find yourself tuning someone out when he or she is boastful or arrogant, or you discern the person is speaking deceitfully? Aren't you more inclined to listen when you sense you're hearing honest words?

I'm not sure God tunes us out when we're trying to impress Him, but I do know that He listens when we bare our souls to Him. Moses, my uncle, and Dorothy are just three examples. Scripture reveals many honest prayers of servants whom God used in dramatic ways.

When Jeremiah's prophesying got him into trouble, he expressed feelings of betrayal in Jeremiah 20:7-10 and succumbed to self-pity in verses 14-18. Even so, God continued to speak to and through Jeremiah and extended his prophetic ministry.

In Habakkuk 1:2, God responded to Habakkuk's complaint—"How long, O LORD, must I call for help, but you do not listen!" The last chapter of Habakkuk leads me to believe that he was satisfied with God's response, although it may not have been exactly what he wanted to hear.

In Mark 15:34, Jesus prayed on the Cross, "My God, my God, why have you forsaken me?" God ultimately responded with resurrection power!

Like Moses, Jeremiah, Habakkuk, Dorothy, my uncle, and Jesus, you, too, can boldly and honestly open your heart to God. He knows already. He's working in your life to bring you to a new level of dependence on Him. Even if it seems to you that He has brought you to the desert to die or has placed you in a leadership role that's killing you, He sees all that lies ahead.

This month, "Pour out your hearts like water to the Lord" (Lamentations 2:19, NLT). But after you do, be sure to listen carefully. You probably won't hear thunder or see lightning bolts, but, as Moses did, you may hear clear directions for what to do next. Or your life may be turned around by one short sentence as my uncle's was. You may receive healing from your brokenness as Dorothy did.

God may say simply, "Do you feel better now that you have that off your chest?"

Even if He remains silent, God's love for you is not diminished by your outburst. You can leave your place of prayer with that peaceful assurance.

Focus for the Month:

Exodus 19-20; 33-34
Numbers 11 and 12
Deuteronomy 5-6; 34
Galatians 3-6

TODAY IS _____

Read Exodus 19

Listen through scripture:

EXODUS 19:3-6:

Then Moses went up to God, and the LORD called to him from the mountain and said, "This is what you are to say to the house of Jacob and what you are to tell the people of Israel: 'You yourselves have seen what I did to Egypt, and how I carried you on eagles' wings and brought you to myself. Now if you obey me fully and keep my covenant, then out of all nations you will be my treasured possession. Although the whole earth is mine, you will be for me a kingdom of priests, and a holy nation.' These are the words you are to speak to the Israelites."

What I sensed God saying to me:

You have seen me work in the past, but it is nothing compared to what I am going to do.

What message is God giving you?

_____

_____

_____

_____

_____

_____

_____

_____

_____

TODAY IS _____

Listen through scripture:

EXODUS 20:16-17:

You shall not give false testimony against your neighbor.

You shall not covet your neighbor's house. You shall not covet your neighbor's wife, or his manservant or maidservant, his ox or donkey, or anything that belongs to your neighbor.

What I sensed God saying to me:

It is in the secret place you find me. Fling the door of your heart open wide, and I will reveal hidden secrets, treasures, and truths that will come only as you quiet yourself before me. Allow me to expose your innermost thoughts. I hear your prayers for your schedule, struggling friends, and life issues. Put these aside, and dwell in my presence.

What message is God giving you?

_____

_____

_____

_____

_____

_____

_____

_____

_____

_____

TODAY IS _____

Listen through scripture:

EXODUS 24:15-18, NLT:

Then Moses climbed up the mountain, and the cloud covered it. And the glory of the LORD settled down on Mount Sinai, and the cloud covered it for six days. On the seventh day the LORD called to Moses from inside the cloud. To the Israelites at the foot of the mountain, the glory of the LORD appeared at the summit like a consuming fire. Then Moses disappeared into the cloud as he climbed higher up the mountain. He remained on the mountain forty days and forty nights.

EXODUS 31:18:

When the Lord finished speaking to Moses on Mount Sinai, he gave him the two tablets of the Testimony, the tablets of stone inscribed by the finger of God.

What I sensed God saying to me:

Pause here to dwell on this thought: "inscribed by the finger of God." What has the finger of God inscribed on the tablets of your heart?

What message is God giving you?

_____

_____

_____

_____

_____

_____

_____

_____

TODAY IS _____

Listen through scripture:

EXODUS 33:12-14, NLT:

One day Moses said to the LORD, "You have been telling me, 'Take these people up to the Promised Land.' But you haven't told me whom you will send with me. You have told me, 'I know you by name, and I look favorably on you.' If it is true that you look favorably on me, let me know your ways so I may understand you more fully and continue to enjoy your favor. And remember that this nation is your very own people."

The LORD replied, "I will personally go with you, Moses, and I will give you rest—everything will be fine for you."

What I sensed God saying to me:

I know your name. I look favorably on you. I will personally go with you wherever I send you. Everything will be fine. Remember—your ideas, love of beauty, and creativity come from me. These are my gifts to you.

What message is God giving you?

_____

_____

_____

_____

_____

_____

_____

_____

_____

_____

TODAY IS _____

Listen through scripture:

EXODUS 34:33-35, NLT:

When Moses finished speaking with them, he covered his face with a veil. But whenever he went into the Tent of Meeting to speak with the LORD, he would remove the veil until he came out again. Then he would give the people whatever instructions the LORD had given him, and the people of Israel would see the radiant glow of his face. So he would put the veil over his face until he returned to speak with the LORD.

What I sensed God saying to me:

When you are still, quiet, and calm, assured that I am your refuge and strength, others around you absorb that disposition and in turn become calmer, more peaceful, more assured. Your very presence affects others just as my very presence affects you. I, in you and through you, touch others whether you are aware of it or not. Just the same, when you're harried, troubled, and agitated, others in your presence are affected adversely. Do you see why these times alone with me are so important? Not only is your life being changed but multitudes of others also. The multiplication effect of my presence is something you cannot possibly comprehend.

What message is God giving you?

_____

_____

_____

_____

_____

_____

_____

_____

_____

TODAY IS _____

Read Numbers 11 and 12

Listen through scripture:

NUMBERS 12:6-8, NLT:

> And the LORD said to them, "Now listen to what I say:
> "If there were prophets among you, I, the LORD, would reveal myself in visions. I would speak to them in dreams. But not with my servant Moses. Of all my house, he is the one I trust. I speak to him face to face, clearly, and not in riddles! He sees the LORD as he is. So why were you not afraid to criticize my servant Moses?"

What I sensed God saying to me:

> Do not criticize—not anything to anyone! What you cannot change, let me use. I expect you to follow this guide in all areas of your life. I don't mean that you can't effect change when given the opportunity, but be very careful with the words you speak, and speak them only when they can make a difference and to the person who can implement the suggestions. Don't burden others with your opinions about past or future events and scheduling. Don't pepper your conversations with disapproving thoughts.

What message is God giving you?

_____

_____

_____

_____

_____

_____

_____

TODAY IS _____

Listen through scripture:

DEUTERONOMY 6:6-7, NLT:

And you must commit yourselves wholeheartedly to these commands that I am giving you today. Repeat them again and again to your children. Talk about them when you are at home and when you are on the road, when you are going to bed and when you are getting up.

What I sensed God saying to me:

Realize that when you are listening to my children, you are listening to me. I will give you wisdom and discernment. Allow me to give you a calm strength that does not panic.

What message is God giving you?

_____

_____

_____

_____

_____

_____

_____

_____

_____

_____

_____

_____

TODAY IS _____

Listen through scripture:

DEUTERONOMY 8:2-3:

Remember how the LORD your God led you all the way in the desert these forty years, to humble you and to test you in order to know what was in your heart, whether or not you would keep his commands. He humbled you, causing you to hunger and then feeding you with manna, which neither you nor your fathers had known, to teach you that man does not live on bread alone but on every word that comes from the mouth of the LORD.

What I sensed God saying to me:

I have heard your prayers for yourself and your pride. It is easy to get into the trap of doing the right things for the wrong motives—prayer, for instance. You have brought these temptations to me, and my Holy Spirit is allowing you to recognize and identify motives of the heart.

What message is God giving you?

_____

_____

_____

_____

_____

_____

_____

_____

_____

_____

TODAY IS _____

Listen through scripture:

DEUTERONOMY 8:11-14:

Be careful that you do not forget the LORD your God, failing to observe his commands, his laws and his decrees that I am giving you this day. Otherwise, when you eat and are satisfied, when you build fine houses and settle down, and when your herds and flocks grow large and your silver and gold increase and all you have is multiplied, then your heart will become proud and you will forget the LORD your God, who brought you out of Egypt, out of the land of slavery.

What I sensed God saying to me:

You are not here to please or impress. Do I have permission to use your failures?

What message is God giving you?

_____

_____

_____

_____

_____

_____

_____

_____

_____

_____

TODAY IS _____

Listen through scripture:

DEUTERONOMY 10:17:

    The LORD your God is God of gods and Lord of lords, the great God, mighty and awesome, who shows no partiality and accepts no bribes.

What I sensed God saying to me:

    Again I ask you, do I have permission to use your failures? Remember—what seems like a failure in your eyes or the eyes of others may not be a failure at all. You can see how many of the burdens you picked up along your journey—both in childhood and in adulthood—seemed to be failures to you. Can you see how I have made creative use of it all?

What message is God giving you?

_____

_____

_____

_____

_____

_____

_____

_____

_____

_____

_____

TODAY IS _____

Listen through scripture:

DEUTERONOMY 32:1-4, NLT:

Listen, O heavens, and I will speak!
Hear, O earth, the words that I say!
Let my teaching fall on you like rain;
let my speech settle like dew.
Let my words fall like rain on tender grass,
like gentle showers on young plants.
I will proclaim the name of the LORD;
how glorious is our God!
He is the Rock; his deeds are perfect.
Everything he does is just and fair.
He is a faithful God who does no wrong;
how just and upright he is!

What I sensed God saying to me:

I want you to have absolute joy every day of your life, but that joy ab-solutely is found in me. I am your hope, your purpose, the seed of your joy. Your relationship with me is the key. It is the key to your inner joy, spreading joy, and your relationship with others. Ask yourself this question often: Does this word or action contribute to someone else's joy?

What message is God giving you?

_____

_____

_____

_____

_____

_____

_____

TODAY IS _____

Listen through scripture:

GALATIANS 2:16, NLT:

We know that a person is made right with God by faith in Jesus Christ, not by obeying the law. And we have believed in Christ Jesus, so that we might be made right with God because of our faith in Christ, not because we have obeyed the law. For no one will ever be made right with God by obeying the law.

What I sensed God saying to me:

Reflect on my provision in the past, and rejoice in my presence today. Expect me to walk beside you into the future. My promises are sure. You have seen my miracles in the past. More are in store. Walk into the future unafraid.

What message is God giving you?

_____

_____

_____

_____

_____

_____

_____

_____

_____

_____

_____

_____

TODAY IS _____

Listen through scripture:

GALATIANS 3:19-21, NLT:

Why, then, was the law given? It was given alongside the promise to show people their sins. But the law was designed to last only until the coming of the child who was promised. God gave his law through angels to Moses, who was the mediator between God and the people. Now a mediator is helpful if more than one party must reach an agreement. But God, who is one, did not use a mediator when he gave his promise to Abraham. Is there a conflict, then, between God's law and God's promises? Absolutely not! If the law could give us new life, we could be made right with God by obeying it. But the Scriptures declare that we are all prisoners of sin before we come to Christ, so we receive God's promise of freedom only by believing in Jesus Christ.

What I sensed God saying to me:

You are wholly mine!

What message is God giving you?

_____

_____

_____

_____

_____

_____

_____

_____

TODAY IS _____

Listen through scripture:

GALATIANS 5:22-26, NLT:

The Holy Spirit produces this kind of fruit in our lives: love, joy, peace, patience, kindness, goodness, faithfulness, gentleness, and self-control. There is no law against these things! Those who belong to Christ Jesus have nailed the passions and desires of their sinful nature to his cross and crucified them there. Since we are living by the Spirit, let us follow the Spirit's leading in every part of our lives.

What I sensed God saying to me:

This will be a significant day. I have everything under control. Be ready for sudden surprise visits of me. You have received the Holy Spirit. Allow the fruit of the Holy Spirit to be evident in your life. Others will see it; you may not. I am guiding now. I am here now.

What message is God giving you?

_____

_____

_____

_____

_____

_____

_____

_____

_____

_____

_____

TODAY IS _____

Listen through scripture:

GALATIANS 6:7-10, NLT:

Don't be misled—you cannot mock the justice of God. You will always harvest what you plant. Those who live only to satisfy their own sinful nature will harvest decay and death from that sinful nature. But those who live to please the Spirit will harvest everlasting life from the Spirit. So let's not get tired of doing what is good. At just the right time we will reap a harvest of blessing if we don't give up. Therefore, whenever we have the opportunity, we should do good to everyone—especially to those in the family of faith.

What I sensed God saying to me:

Be strong and take heart as you put your hope in me. Pull back. Refrain from cluttering your day. When you sense yourself becoming tense or anxious, step back into my presence. Spend the day with me. As you give of yourself and your time with others, do it as if unto me.

What message is God giving you?

_____

_____

_____

_____

_____

_____

_____

_____

_____

With an honest, open heart, Moses continued to lead the Israelites for 40 years in spite of the heartbreaking news from God early in the journey that another leader would take the Israelites into the Promised Land.

What lessons have you learned from the life of Moses?

Pause to bare your soul to the Lord, and be sure both to listen and to watch carefully for God's response.

LISTENING WITH ENLIGHTENED EYES

Since his youth Joshua had been Moses' assistant. He followed Moses' instructions and fought the army of Amalek as Moses held up his staff. When Moses' arms grew tired, Aaron and Hur found a stone for Moses to sit on, and they stood on each side, holding up his hands until sunset. "As a result, Joshua overwhelmed the army of Amalek in battle" (Exodus 17:13, NLT).

When God called Moses to come up on the mountain with tablets of stone, "Moses and his assistant Joshua set out, and Moses climbed up the mountain of God" (Exodus 24:13, NLT). In Exodus 32:15-18 we learn that when Moses returned from the mountain, Joshua was with him.

Joshua was at the Tent of Meeting when Moses spoke with God:

> Inside the Tent of Meeting, the LORD would speak to Moses face to face, as one speaks to a friend. Afterward Moses would return to the camp, but the young man who assisted him, Joshua son of Nun, would remain behind in the Tent of Meeting *(Exodus 33:11, NLT).*

Joshua was one of the 12 tribal leaders Moses sent as scouts to explore Canaan with specific instructions:

> When Moses sent them to explore Canaan, he said, "Go up through the Negev and on into the hill country. See what the land is like and whether the people who live there are strong or weak, few or many. What kind of land do they live in? Is it good or bad? What kind of towns do they live in? Are they unwalled or fortified? How is the soil? Is it fertile or poor? Are there trees on it or not? Do your best to bring back some of the fruit of the land." It was the season for the first ripe grapes *(Numbers 13:17-20).*

The explorers returned with a cluster of grapes so large that it took two men to carry it back. They also brought samples of pomegranates and figs, reporting that the land was beautiful. Even with this glowing report, 10 tribal leaders saw giants and intimidating circumstances and compared themselves to grasshoppers. Joshua and Caleb saw possibilities and wanted to go at once to conquer and take over the land. They pleaded with the despairing Israelites and tried to convince them to proceed. (See Numbers 14:8-9.)

The Israelites' disbelief in God's power to help them conquer the land resulted in their wandering in the wilderness for 40 years. God denied them, along with Moses, the privilege of entering the Promised Land; the only exceptions were Joshua and Caleb.

God chose Joshua to be Moses' successor. Moses, at the end of his life, gave Joshua a charge. In Deuteronomy 3:21-28, he commissioned him to lead the people across the Jordan River.

When Moses had finished giving these instructions to all the people of Israel, he said, "I am now 120 years old, and I am no longer able to lead you. The LORD has told me, 'You will not cross the Jordan River.' But the LORD your God himself will cross over ahead of you. He will destroy the nations living there, and you will take possession of their land. Joshua will lead you across the river, just as the LORD promised" *(Deuteronomy 31:1-3, NLT).*

Then Moses summoned Joshua and said to him in the presence of all Israel. "Be strong and courageous, for you must go with this people into the land that the LORD swore to their forefathers to give them, and you must divide it among them as their inheritance. The LORD himself goes before you and will be with you; he will never leave you nor forsake you. Do not be afraid; do not be discouraged" *(Deuteronomy 31:7-8).*

• • • • • •

I had accepted the position as children's director for our church but was confident that God was calling me to this assignment for only one year. Although it was a volunteer position, there were approximately 50 workers under my leadership, and some weeks I spent that many hours on the job. I chose a preschool and an elementary coordinator to assist me. Both ladies knew that I was preparing them to take over full responsibilities the following year. However, the elementary coordinator moved to another state; the preschool coordinator's husband accepted a major leadership position in the church, and she felt she should assist him

It looked as if no one was willing to accept the role of children's ministries director. But then the second-grade Sunday School teacher, Sandy, volunteered to fill in until someone permanent could be found. Without re-alizing it, she was being trained by God for the position as she worked alongside me throughout the year. She attended all the meetings and helped with every event.

Sandy had assisted me in starting the puppet team and eventually led that ministry. We worked together on Vacation Bible School. Her son was one of the main characters in the Christmas drama and musical, and she was there for every practice, assisting and helping design animal costumes. She came to all the parties and helped with every field trip.

After a few months, no one else had stepped up to become the direc-tor of children's ministries, and Sandy volunteered once again. She became an outstanding, creative leader. Like Joshua, Sandy was being trained; how-ever, neither one of us knew it. God has taught me through this experience and others that when He tells me no, He has someone else that He is preparing to do His work—a Joshua.

● ● ● ● ● ● ●

I most remember Joshua from the childhood story and song about Jericho:

Around the walls of Jericho
The Israelites would daily go.
The seventh day the walls gave way,
And they came tumbling down.

The children then fall down as if we are the tumbling walls.

I reread the Battle of Jericho story in Joshua 6 when loved ones were facing a crisis, and I cried out to God. I decided to fast and focus my prayers on this need for seven days.

I sat down with my journal and asked God to reveal to me the walls that needed to come down in that particular relationship. He gave me a long list, and I began to pray that those specific walls would crumble. Strange as it may seem, I decided to walk around my dining room table once each day, naming the walls and praying that they would be demol-ished.

The seventh day I circled the table seven times, ending with a shout and a victory prayer. From that point I tried to only praise God for hearing my prayers and removing the walls, although it appeared that new walls were being erected and matters were worse.

Then I received an unexpected phone call. It was as if the walls had crumbled miraculously—overnight! Relationships were restored, and God continues His work in the lives of those dear ones.

I have been hesitant to share that story because I was afraid the real point of it would be missed. The significance here was getting direction from God on how to pray. We often bluster into God's presence with our needs and prayers without getting His perspective on the issue. Not so with Joshua.

When Joshua was near the town of Jericho, he looked up and saw a man standing in front of him with sword in hand. Joshua went up to him and demanded, "Are you friend or foe?"

"Neither one," he replied. "I am the commander of the LORD's army."

At this, Joshua fell with his face to the ground in reverence. "I am at your command," Joshua said. "What do you want your servant to do?"

The commander of the LORD's army replied, "Take off your sandals, for the place where you are standing is holy." And Joshua did as he was told (*Joshua 5:13-15, NLT*).

How do we develop eyes to see from God's perspective? In John 4:35 Jesus told His disciples to wake up and look around.

Then Jesus explained, "My nourishment comes from doing the will of God, who sent me, and from finishing his work. You know the saying, 'Four months between planting and harvest.' But I say, wake up and look around. The fields are already ripe for harvest" (*vv. 34-35, NLT*).

In Matthew 9 Jesus not only told His disciples what He saw but also advised them on how to turn that awareness into prayer.

Jesus traveled through all the towns and villages of that area, teaching in the synagogues and announcing the Good News about the Kingdom. And he healed every kind of disease and illness. When he saw the crowds, he had compassion on them because they were confused and helpless, like sheep without a shepherd. He said to his disciples, "The harvest is great, but the workers are few. So pray to the Lord who is in charge of the harvest; ask him to send more workers into his fields" (*vv. 35-38, NLT*).

In John 9, after He healed the man blind from birth, Jesus spoke about spiritual blindness.

Then Jesus told him, "I entered this world to render judgment—to give sight to the blind and to show those who think they see that they are blind" (v. *39, NLT*).

When we ask God to show us what He sees, and we listen with willing spirits, He will reveal things to us we would not otherwise see, opening our blinded eyes and giving us discernment on how to pray. While the disciples possibly saw only fields beside the road and distracting crowds, Jesus saw fields ripe with harvest and compared it to individuals needing help and spiritual eyes to see.

What do you see? Impossibilities? Your limitations? Or do you see potential and His strength?

This is what Joshua saw:

- Fire on the mountain when God gave Moses the Law
- Radiance on Moses' face when he had spoken with the Lord
- Enormous grapes and a land flowing with milk and honey
- The Jericho walls tumbling
- Many battles won in the Lord's strength
- God's power revealed in outstanding ways.

What do you see?

- Just trees, or oaks, redbuds, birches, and willows
- Just birds, or robins, sparrows, hawks, and finches
- Just people, or individuals—hurting, empty, lonely, hungry, despairing men and women who have lost their way, confused teens searching for answers, children with no one to teach them to take their hurts to Jesus, each one created by God and loved by Him

Look! The fields are ripe for harvest.

Ask God to allow you to see the world through His eyes.

As you pray this month, place the person or need before God. Then wait, listening for Him to direct your prayers. I keep a journal and write down the ways He leads me to pray and the insights He gives. God often guides me to pray scripture for myself and others. Keep your eyes open, and pray the Word aloud.

"To pray Scriptures aloud strengthens our prayers in two ways. First, it focuses our attention. When we pray silently, our prayers are apt to be interrupted by those pesky thoughts that bounce around inside our heads. But once we give our prayers volume, they gain a stronger life and focus."[1]

Pray Ephesians 1:17-23 aloud daily for yourself and someone else.

Focus for the Month:

Joshua 1-6 and 23-24
Ephesians 1
Matthew 6

TODAY IS _____

Listen through scripture:

EPHESIANS 1:17-18:

I keep asking that the God of our Lord Jesus Christ, the glorious Father, may give you the Spirit of wisdom and revelation, so that you may know him better. I pray also that the eyes of your heart may be enlightened in order that you may know the hope to which he has called you, the riches of his glorious inheritance in the saints, and his incomparably great power for us who believe.

What I sensed God saying to me:

Worship me with your every act today. Honor me in the words you speak, the songs you sing, the attitudes of your heart, your actions of grace to others. I want to work and overcome barriers to my Spirit flow.

What message is God giving you?

_____

_____

_____

_____

_____

_____

_____

_____

_____

_____

_____

TODAY IS _____

Read Joshua 1

Listen through scripture:

JOSHUA 1:1-2, 5:

> *After the death of Moses the servant of the* LORD, *the* LORD *said to Joshua son of Nun, Moses' aide: "Moses my servant is dead. Now then, you and all these people, get ready to cross the Jordan River into the land I am about to give to them—to the Israelites" (vv. 1-2). "No one will be able to stand up against you all the days of your life. As I was with Moses, so I will be with you; I will never leave you nor forsake you" (v. 5).*

What I sensed God saying to me:

> *Follow the directives from past listening times that you have bypassed. Remember—Moses and Joshua received directions right down to every minute detail.*

What message is God giving you?

_____

_____

_____

_____

_____

_____

_____

_____

_____

_____

TODAY IS _____

Listen through scripture:

JOSHUA 1:8-9:

Do not let this Book of the Law depart from your mouth; meditate on it day and night, so that you may be careful to do everything written in it. Then you will be prosperous and successful. Have I not commanded you? Be strong and courageous. Do not be terrified; do not be discouraged, for the LORD your God will be with you wherever you go.

What I sensed God saying to me:

Listen for my whispers. Listen for my voice in scripture. Listen to nature, my creation. Sometimes my message will come to you in a shout, unmistakable, audible, clear. However it comes, obey without hesitation.

What message is God giving you?

_____

_____

_____

_____

_____

_____

_____

_____

_____

_____

_____

TODAY IS _____

Read Joshua 3

Listen through scripture:

JOSHUA 3:7:

And the LORD said to Joshua, "Today I will begin to exalt you in the eyes of all Israel, so they may know that I am with you as I was with Moses. Tell the priests who carry the ark of the covenant: 'When you reach the edge of the Jordan's waters, go and stand in the river.'"

What I sensed God saying to me:

Find strength in this quiet place and confidence in me. Find truth in my word; hope in my faithfulness; security in my love; forgiveness in my mercy. Find me in your heart. All these gifts and more are mine to you. All these gifts and more are yours to share with others.

What message is God giving you?

_____

_____

_____

_____

_____

_____

_____

_____

_____

_____

_____

TODAY IS _____

Listen through scripture:

JOSHUA 3:14-17:

When the people broke camp to cross the Jordan, the priests carrying the ark of the covenant went ahead of them. Now the Jordan is at flood stage all during harvest. Yet as soon as the priests who carried the ark reached the Jordan and their feet touched the water's edge, the water from upstream stopped flowing. It piled up in a heap a great distance away, at a town called Adam in the vicinity of Zarethan, while the water flowing down to the Sea of the Arabah the Salt Sea was completely cut off. So the people crossed over opposite Jericho. The priests who carried the ark of the covenant of the LORD stood firm on dry ground in the middle of the Jordan, while all Israel passed by until the whole nation had completed the crossing on dry ground.

What I sensed God saying to me:

I will never leave you. I will always be with you, surrounding you with my holy presence. Above all else, seek me in all circumstances. I realize that I am stretching your faith at this time.

What message is God giving you?

_____

_____

_____

_____

_____

_____

_____

_____

_____

TODAY IS _____

Read Joshua 2 and 6

Listen through scripture:

JOSHUA 6:1-5, NLT:

Now the gates of Jericho were tightly shut because the people were afraid of the Israelites. No one was allowed to go out or in. But the LORD said to Joshua, "I have given you Jericho, its king, and all its strong warriors. You and your fighting men should march around the town once a day for six days. Seven priests will walk ahead of the Ark, each carrying a ram's horn. On the seventh day you are to march around the town seven times, with the priests blowing the horns. When you hear the priests give one long blast on the rams' horns, have all the people shout as loud as they can. Then the walls of the town will collapse, and the people can charge straight into the town."

What I sensed God saying to me:

Learn from me daily. Do not try to live today on yesterday's revelation. Bathe your heart in my presence so that when you go forth, others will know you have been with me. It will not be something you force on others. It will not be you trying to make an impression. It will simply happen as a result of my Spirit flowing through you and spilling onto others.

What message is God giving you?

_____

_____

_____

_____

_____

_____

_____

TODAY IS _____

Read Joshua 23-24

Listen through scripture:

JOSHUA 24:14-15:

Now fear the LORD and serve him with all faithfulness. Throw away the gods your forefathers worshiped beyond the River and in Egypt, and serve the LORD. But if serving the LORD seems undesirable to you, then choose for yourselves this day whom you will serve, whether the gods of your forefathers served beyond the River, or the gods of the Amorites, in whose land you are living. But as for me and my household, we will serve the LORD.

What I sensed God saying to me:

I have been waiting for channels who are willing to be made uncomfortable for me. Remember how I taught in the synagogues but had to take my teachings to the seashore and hillsides because they were not welcome in the Temple. I am looking for men and women who are willing to break out of their comfort zones of the known into a walk by faith, not by sight. You're asking how. Leave that to me. Be obedient in the little directives I give you, and I will take care of the big picture.

What message is God giving you?

_____

_____

_____

_____

_____

_____

_____

TODAY IS _____

Listen through scripture:

JOSHUA 24:16-18:

> *Then the people answered, "Far be it from us to forsake the LORD to serve other gods. It was the LORD our God himself who brought us and our fathers up out of Egypt, from that land of slavery, and performed those great signs before our eyes. He protected us on our entire journey and among all the nations through which we traveled. And the LORD drove out before us all the nations, including the Amorites, who lived in the land. We too will serve the LORD, because he is our God."*

What I sensed God saying to me:

> *Take the message to your world in the ways I lead you. Go forward unafraid, depending completely on me. Live life to the full. Love. Rejoice.*

What message is God giving you?

_____

_____

_____

_____

_____

_____

_____

_____

_____

_____

_____

TODAY IS _____

Listen through scripture:

MATTHEW 6:19-21, NLT:

Don't store up treasures here on earth, where moths eat them and rust destroys them, and where thieves break in and steal. Store your treasures in heaven, where moths and rust cannot destroy and thieves do not break in and steal. Wherever your treasure is, there the desires of your heart will also be.

What I sensed God saying to me:

Keep your life in order so that you can freely do my bidding at a moment's notice.

What message is God giving you?

_____

_____

_____

_____

_____

_____

_____

_____

_____

_____

_____

_____

_____

TODAY IS _____

Listen through scripture:

MATTHEW 6:23, NLT:

But when your eye is bad, your whole body is filled with darkness. And if the light you think you have is actually darkness, how deep that darkness is!

What I sensed God saying to me:

No great work is done for me without struggle and onslaughts from the enemy. Remember that I am the victor.

What message is God giving you?

_____

_____

_____

_____

_____

_____

_____

_____

_____

_____

_____

_____

_____

_____

_____

_____

TODAY IS _____

Listen through scripture:

MATTHEW 6:25:

Therefore I tell you, do not worry about your life, what you will eat or drink; or about your body, what you will wear. Is not life more important than food, and the body more important than clothes? Look at the birds of the air; they do not sow or reap or store away in barns, and yet your heavenly Father feeds them. Are you not much more valuable than they? Who of you by worrying can add a single hour to his life.?

What I sensed God saying to me:

Let me plan your day. You are feeling pressure about things that are not urgent. Keep your life uncluttered.

What message is God giving you?

_____

_____

_____

_____

_____

_____

_____

_____

_____

_____

_____

_____

TODAY IS _____

Listen through scripture:

MATTHEW 6:28, NLT:

And why worry about your clothing? Look at the lilies of the field and how they grow. They don't work or make their clothing, yet Solomon in all his glory was not dressed as beautifully as they are. And if God cares so wonderfully for wildflowers that are here today and thrown into the fire tomorrow, he will certainly care for you. Why do you have so little faith?

What I sensed God saying to me:

Today is a day for rejoicing, a day for celebration, a day for thanksgiving, a day of blessing, a day of prayer. I am sending you as a source of hope to someone today. You do not have to know who it is.

What message is God giving you?

_____

_____

_____

_____

_____

_____

_____

_____

_____

_____

_____

_____

TODAY IS _____

Listen through scripture:

EPHESIANS 5:10-12, NLT:

Carefully determine what pleases the Lord. Take no part in the worthless deeds of evil and darkness; instead, expose them. It is shameful even to talk about the things that ungodly people do in secret. But their evil intentions will be exposed when the light shines on them, for the light makes everything visible. This is why it is said, "Awake, O sleeper, rise up from the dead, and Christ will give you light."

What I sensed God saying to me:

Be present in mind and spirit for each task set before you.

What message is God giving you?

_____

_____

_____

_____

_____

_____

_____

_____

_____

_____

_____

_____

_____

TODAY IS _____

Listen through scripture:

EPHESIANS 6:13-17, NLT:

> *Therefore, put on every piece of God's armor so you will be able to resist the enemy in the time of evil. Then after the battle you will still be standing firm. Stand your ground, putting on the belt of truth and the body armor of God's righteousness. For shoes, put on the peace that comes from the Good News so that you will be fully prepared. In addition to all of these, hold up the shield of faith to stop the fiery arrows of the devil. Put on salvation as your helmet, and take the sword of the Spirit, which is the word of God.*

What I sensed God saying to me:

> *Live in my Word. Follow truth.*

What message is God giving you?

_____

_____

_____

_____

_____

_____

_____

_____

_____

_____

_____

TODAY IS _____

Listen through scripture:

LUKE 10:23:

    Then he turned to his disciples and said privately, "Blessed are the eyes that see what you see."

What I sensed God saying to me:

    Take pleasure in each stage of your life. Turn your moaning into praise and your groaning into expressions of delight. No one enjoys hearing complaints. Open your eyes; behold me.

What message is God giving you?

_____

_____

_____

_____

_____

_____

_____

_____

_____

_____

_____

_____

_____

Has your spiritual vision improved this month?

- Go outside and observe things you have never noticed before.
- Look into the eyes of everyone you meet today. Give them a smile from God, and breathe a prayer for any area of spiritual darkness that needs illumination.
- Ask God to give you a vision of how He wants you to participate in His work.
- Allow God to continue revealing His power and glory, giving you divine eyesight and holy illumination as you unfold your hands to serve Him in any way He leads.

LISTENING WITH OPEN HANDS

Read 1 Samuel 1 through 3. I frequently use Hannah's story from these chapters as a model for prayer. In chapter 1, verses 3-8, notice Hannah's husband, Elkanah. He is a devout, religious man who led his family to faithfully worship God. He cared for his family; and he loved Hannah and was compassionate.

Stop here to pray for men in your family and church. Pray that they will be Psalm 1 men, who don't follow the advice of the wicked but delight in the Scriptures and meditate on God's Word day and night—men who are like sturdy trees planted by the river bearing fruit, prospering, seeking God for direction.

In verses 9-18 we learn that Hannah was in deep anguish because she had no children, and she poured her heart out to God, asking for a son. She promised to give him back to God and dedicate him to the Lord. When Eli saw her lips moving but making no sound, he accused her of being drunk. This did not deter her—she was desperate. When she explained to Eli that she was pouring out her heart to God, he softened and extended a blessing to her. "'In that case,' Eli said, 'go in peace! May the God of Israel grant the request you have asked of him'" (1 Samuel 1:17, NLT). Hannah was no longer downcast and sad.

Do you feel as bad or worse after you have prayed? The reason may be that you have focused on the problem rather than God's ability to answer. What are you desperate about? Give God your hugest request, the one only He can fix.

There are reasons Hannah left her place of prayer with the burden lifted. She went to the right source, and she poured out her need to God honestly and specifically. She promised to give the answer back to God. She shared her burden with Eli, and then she left the request with God, knowing that He had heard.

God answered, and Samuel was born. Hannah kept her promise and gave him to the Lord as an act of worship. Now, many centuries later, my life has been changed by Hannah's prayer. Several years ago while reading her story, I became intrigued by the thought of giving the answers back to God.

- *How do we give answers back to you, God?*
- *Please show me, God, what you want to teach me about this concept.*

I'm learning that one prayer leads to the next prayer; any answer or part of the answer opens the way for another prayer. I feel confident that Hannah's prayers for Samuel deepened after she left him at the Temple and continued after each annual visit.

● ● ● ● ● ●

A dear friend of mine was praying that her husband would begin attending church with her again. As she and her young son were driving to church one Sunday, the toddler, who loved going to church and hearing the music, cried, saying, "Daddy go church with you." She stopped the car, and they prayed.

Her prayer partner advised her to pray for herself during this period and ask God to prepare her for the day her husband would become totally sold out to Jesus. This wise young lady warned my friend that her life could radically change if God called her husband into ministry or if he became committed beyond what she was ready to accept. My friend entered a period of praying for God to prepare her for what was ahead.

Eventually her husband agreed to return to church if they went to a church with a different style of worship. My friend agreed. At the new church, the pastor preached powerful biblical sermons, but it seemed as if the people were unresponsive and attending more from tradition than passion.

Every week my friend gave the answer back to God, and one Sunday she asked God, *If this is where I am to be, please let me see that someone is happy to be here.* At the close of the service, the instrumentalists played the song they played every week as a recessional. That particular Sunday alone, someone started clapping, and the entire congregation spontaneously joined in and clapped on the way out of the sanctuary!

The next week she prayed, *It's obvious that this pastor is a man of prayer, but do any of his people pray? I must be a part of a praying church. Please let me know that there is at least one other praying person in this church.* When the offering was collected, the pastor called on an usher to pray. This was no ordinary offering prayer. The man began to weep and plead with God for the church and the salvation of the lost.

Every week her husband attended church with her and their son, and each week my friend gave God's answer back to Him. That's the way prayer works. We ask, we receive, we give the answer back to God, and we formulate another prayer. There's no finality in the answer—it keeps going.

What if God answers your prayers? Are you ready for how that might totally change the direction of your life? Are you prepared to give the answer back to God with open hands?

• • • • • •

I wonder how many times, how many years, Hannah prayed for a son. Scripture gives only one account, but she may have prayed hundreds or thousands of times, receiving what seemed to her to be no response. She did not give up. Was this the first time she had promised to give the answer back to God? We don't know. What we do know is that she persisted in prayer, kept her commitment, and her prayer was answered. The Lord then used His answer to provide a leader who brought glory to God throughout all of Israel—and the results continue eternally!

• • • • • •

What does God have in His hands? Speaking of Zion, God said, "See, I have your name written on the palms of my hands" (Isaiah 49:16, NLT). No doubt your name and mine are written there too. In Psalm 50:12 the Lord tells us that the world and everything in it are His.

This month focus on using your hands to bless and opening them to release and praise.

"In every place of worship, I want men to pray with holy hands lifted up to God, free from anger and controversy" (1 Timothy 2:8, NLT).

Focus for the Month:

1 Samuel

TODAY IS _____

Listen through scripture:

I SAMUEL 3:2-5:

One night Eli, whose eyes were becoming so weak that he could barely see, was lying down in his usual place. The lamp of God had not yet gone out, and Samuel was lying down in the temple of the LORD, where the ark of God was. Then the LORD called Samuel. Samuel answered, "Here I am." And he ran to Eli and said, "Here I am; you called me." But Eli said, "I did not call; go back and lie down." So he went and lay down.

What I sensed God saying to me:

I am at work even when I am silent. Trust me in the silence; trust me in the darkness. Trust me and not circumstances even in the light.

What message is God giving you?

_____

_____

_____

_____

_____

_____

_____

_____

_____

_____

_____

_____

TODAY IS _____

Listen through scripture:

I SAMUEL 3:8-9:

The LORD called Samuel a third time, and Samuel got up and went to Eli and said, "Here I am; you called me." Then Eli realized that the LORD was calling the boy. So Eli told Samuel, "Go and lie down, and if he calls you, say, 'Speak, LORD, for your servant is listening.'" So Samuel went and lay down in his place.

What I sensed God saying to me:

Keep your eyes on me—on the goal—always focused away from self and others, away from obstacles and circumstances, straight ahead. Do not turn to the left or right without orders from me. Keep your gaze upward.

What message is God giving you?

_____

_____

_____

_____

_____

_____

_____

_____

_____

_____

_____

_____

TODAY IS _____

Listen through scripture:

I SAMUEL 3:10-11:

The LORD came and stood there, calling as at the other times, "Samuel! Samuel!"

Then Samuel said, "Speak, for your servant is listening."

And the LORD said to Samuel: "See, I am about to do something in Israel that will make the ears of everyone who hear of it tingle."

What I sensed God saying to me:

Do not take things too personally. Do not hold grudges when people do not live up to your expectations. Remember that many times you do not live up to the expectations of others.

What message is God giving you?

_____

_____

_____

_____

_____

_____

_____

_____

_____

_____

_____

TODAY IS _____

Listen through scripture:

I SAMUEL 3:20-21, NLT:

And all Israel, from Dan in the north to Beersheba in the south, knew that Samuel was confirmed as a prophet of the LORD. The LORD continued to appear at Shiloh and gave messages to Samuel there at the Tabernacle. And Samuel's words went out to all the people of Israel.

What I sensed God saying to me:

When you recognize traits in yourself that you don't like, hand them to me. Let me remove, replace, repair, or revitalize as I see fit. Just the act of recognizing and relinquishing is redemptive material for me to mold or remold.

What message is God giving you?

_____

_____

_____

_____

_____

_____

_____

_____

_____

_____

_____

_____

TODAY IS _____

Listen through scripture:

I SAMUEL 7:3:

And Samuel said to the whole house of Israel, "If you are returning to the LORD with all your hearts, then rid yourselves of the foreign gods and the Ashtoreths and commit yourselves to the LORD and serve him only, and he will deliver you out of the hand of the Philistines."

What I sensed God saying to me:

Do not rush me. Do not put undue pressure on yourself. Do not place unnecessary pressure on others. Yet, I want you to obey me even when it makes you uncomfortable.

What message is God giving you?

_____

_____

_____

_____

_____

_____

_____

_____

_____

_____

_____

_____

TODAY IS _____

Read 1 Samuel 8

Listen through scripture:

I SAMUEL 8:1-3, NLT:

As Samuel grew old, he appointed his sons to be judges over Israel. Joel and Abijah, his oldest sons, held court in Beersheba. But they were not like their father, for they were greedy for money. They accepted bribes and perverted justice.

What I sensed God saying to me:

When you are teaching, you may at times be led by me to ask others to do things that stretch them out of their comfort zone. Be sure it is for their good and is God-directed.

What message is God giving you?

_____

_____

_____

_____

_____

_____

_____

_____

_____

_____

TODAY IS _____

Listen through scripture:

I SAMUEL 8:4-5, NLT:

Finally, all the elders of Israel met at Ramah to discuss the matter with Samuel. "Look," they told him, "you are now old, and your sons are not like you. Give us a king to judge us like all the other nations have."

What I sensed God saying to me:

My name uttered in praise brings joy. My name spoken in times of fear brings peace. My name cried out in pain brings healing. My name called upon in time of need brings wholeness. My name revered envelopes you with awe. My name spoken in discord brings new understanding. My name claimed when rejected brings acceptance. Speak my name often this day.

What message is God giving you?

_____

_____

_____

_____

_____

_____

_____

_____

_____

_____

_____

TODAY IS _____

Listen through scripture:

I SAMUEL 8:6-9, NLT:

Samuel was displeased with their request and went to the LORD for guidance. "Do everything they say to you," the LORD replied, "for it is me they are rejecting, not you. They don't want me to be their king any longer. Ever since I brought them from Egypt they have continually abandoned me and followed other gods. And now they are giving you the same treatment. Do as they ask, but solemnly warn them about the way a king will reign over them."

What I sensed God saying to me:

Keep expanding your prayer life. Expand your horizons. Expand your heart to include all I send your way. Expand your mind. Enlarge your vision.

What message is God giving you?

_____

_____

_____

_____

_____

_____

_____

_____

_____

_____

_____

_____

TODAY IS _____

Read Samuel 10

Listen through scripture:

I SAMUEL 10:1, NLT:

Then Samuel took a flask of olive oil and poured it over Saul's head. He kissed Saul and said, "I am doing this because the LORD has appointed you to be the ruler over Israel, his special possession.

What I sensed God saying to me:

Go where I send you. Do not try to put a label on my assignments. Take them as they come, big or small, adventuresome or mundane, glamorous or demeaning. Any work done in my name is mighty. Do not evaluate by the few or many, young or aged, leader or follower. Do all for my sake alone, not for fame or fortune, comfort and ease; just do all I command because I have spoken and given you my call.

What message is God giving you?

_____

_____

_____

_____

_____

_____

_____

_____

_____

_____

TODAY IS _____

Read 1 Samuel 12

Listen through scripture:

I SAMUEL 12:1-2:

Samuel said to all Israel, "I have listened to everything you said to me and have set a king over you. Now you have a king as your leader. As for me, I am old and gray, and my sons are here with you. I have been your leader from my youth until this day."

What I sensed God saying to me:

I speak your name often, in tenderness and joy, in love and acceptance, in forgiveness and delight. I take joy in sending you blessings, but sometimes I allow struggles to teach you.

What message is God giving you?

_____

_____

_____

_____

_____

_____

_____

_____

_____

_____

TODAY IS _____

Listen through scripture:

I SAMUEL 13:1 AND 15:10:

Saul was thirty years old when he became king, and he reigned over Israel forty-two years (13:1).

Then the word of the LORD came to Samuel: "I am grieved that I have made Saul king, because he has turned away from me and has not carried out my instructions." Samuel was troubled, and he cried out to the LORD all that night (15:10).

What I sensed God saying to me:

It is very dangerous to step out of my will. Many leaders who have been called by me become ineffective when they fail to remain open to my leading in all matters.

What message is God giving you?

_____

_____

_____

_____

_____

_____

_____

_____

_____

_____

TODAY IS _____

Listen through scripture:

I SAMUEL 15:22-23, NLT:

But Samuel replied, *"What is more pleasing to the LORD: your burnt of-ferings and sacrifices or your obedience to his voice? Listen! Obedience is better than sacrifice, and submission is better than offering the fat of rams. Rebellion is as sinful as witchcraft, and stubbornness as bad as worshiping idols. So be-cause you have rejected the command of the LORD, he has rejected you as king."*

What I sensed God saying to me:

I see that you are longing to make a difference in your world. I see your openness to changes I want to make in your heart and life. I see your wish for every word you speak to have eternal impact for good. Take me with you everywhere you go, and these prayers will be answered.

What message is God giving you?

_____

_____

_____

_____

_____

_____

_____

_____

_____

_____

TODAY IS _____

Listen through scripture:

I SAMUEL 15:35-16:1:

Until the day Samuel died, he did not go to see Saul again, though Samuel mourned for him. And the LORD was grieved that he had made Saul king over Israel. The LORD said to Samuel, "How long will you mourn for Saul, since I have rejected him as king over Israel? Fill your horn with oil and be on your way; I am sending you to Jesse of Bethlehem. I have chosen one of his sons to be king."

What I sensed God saying to me:

Do not spread gloom to your world and those around you.

What message is God giving you?

_____

_____

_____

_____

_____

_____

_____

_____

_____

_____

_____

_____

_____

TODAY IS _____

Listen through scripture:

I SAMUEL 16:6-7:

When they arrived, Samuel saw Eliab and thought, "Surely the LORD's anointed stands here before the LORD." But the LORD said to Samuel, "Do not consider his appearance or his height, for I have rejected him. The LORD does not look at the things man looks at. Man looks at the outward appearance, but the LORD looks at the heart."

What I sensed God saying to me:

I am bringing healing to multitudes of my emotionally crippled children who have been harmed by evil men and women. Keep believing! Keep trusting!

What message is God giving you?

_____

_____

_____

_____

_____

_____

_____

_____

_____

_____

_____

_____

TODAY IS _____

Listen through scripture:

I SAMUEL 16:10-13:

Jesse had seven of his sons pass before Samuel, but Samuel said to him, "The LORD has not chosen these." So he asked Jesse, "Are these all the sons you have?"

"There is still the youngest," Jesse answered, "but he is tending the sheep."

Samuel said, "Send for him; we will not sit down until he arrives."

So he sent and had him brought in. He was ruddy, with a fine appearance and handsome features.

Then the LORD said, "Rise and anoint him; he is the one."

So Samuel took the horn of oil and anointed him in the presence of his brothers, and from that day on the Spirit of the LORD came upon David in power.

What I sensed God saying to me:

Are you ready for my next assignment? Do not recoil in fear. Come forward joyfully to receive my orders. I will give you strength and peace of heart. May I have your day and your full attention?

What message is God giving you?

_____

_____

_____

_____

_____

_____

_____

_____

Did you follow Hannah's example as you prayed this month? Did God call your name in the night hours? And did you respond, "Speak, Lord, for I am listening!" as Eli instructed Samuel to do?

Samuel continued throughout his lifetime to listen to God, and in his farewell speech he said,

> As for me, I will certainly not sin against the LORD by ending my prayers for you. And I will continue to teach you what is good and right. But be sure to fear the LORD and faithfully serve him. Think of all the wonderful things he has done for you *(1 Samuel 12:23-24, NLT)*.

Give thanks that someone penned the story of Hannah and Samuel.

LISTENING WITH PEN IN HAND

We would not have one verse of Scripture preserved for our reading if God had not instructed His servants to write their stories and His messages to them. Scripture tells us that God told Moses, Joshua, Jeremiah, Habbakuk, John, and others to write things He wanted us to know and remember.

When Joshua and the Israeli army defeated the Amalekites after they attacked the Israelites at Rephidim, God instructed Moses to write the account on a scroll to be remembered:

Then the LORD said to Moses, "Write this on a scroll as something to be remembered and make sure that Joshua hears it" *(Exodus 17:14).*

Moses obeyed.

When the Lord told Moses that He was making a covenant and would do wonders never before done in any nation in the world, He instructed Moses to write down His words.

Then the LORD said to Moses, "Write down these words, for in accordance with these words I have made a covenant with you and with Israel" *(Exodus 34:27).*

In Deuteronomy, before turning over leadership to Joshua, Moses gave a summary of the Israelites' journey to the Promised Land and mentions that the Lord told him to write. "Now write down for yourselves this song, and teach it to the Israelites and have them sing it, so that it may be a witness for me against them" (Deuteronomy 31:19).

"So Moses wrote down this song that day and taught it to the Israelites" (Deuteronomy 31:22).

After Moses finished writing the entire body of instructions in a book, he commanded it to be placed beside the ark of the covenant of the Lord. (See Deuteronomy 31:24-26.)

In Joshua 24:26 we are told that Joshua also kept records.

Besides historical stories and God's commands being recorded by Moses, Joshua, and others, the prophets were prompted by God to write His messages to be delivered.

Jeremiah 36 tells the story of the Lord instructing the prophet Jeremiah to write on a scroll the words given to him for Israel. Jeremiah dictated the words to a scribe named Baruch and instructed him to read the scroll aloud in the Temple. King Jehoiakim had the scroll burned when he learned of this. Jeremiah would not be deterred from doing what the Lord had instructed and had the scroll rewritten. That message, combined with supplements, is still available for our reading today!

Many chapters of the book of Jeremiah are filled with dismal warnings sprinkled with a bright promise here and there. Of these promises quoted from Jeremiah, the one I most often hear, is "'I know the plans I have for you,' declares the LORD, 'plans to prosper you and not to harm you, plans to give you hope and a future'" (Jeremiah 29:11).

These words were written to the people in exile, telling them it would be 70 years before they would be allowed to return from Babylon to their homeland, contrary to what false prophets were predicting. The most important part of that passage is often left unquoted: "Then you will call upon me and come and pray to me, and I will listen to you. You will seek me and find me when you seek me with all your heart" (Jeremiah 29:12-13).

What message might God be asking you to write to share with others? A poem, song, story, letter, or book? An abundance of Christian literature is at our fingertips, because God still calls His children to write. Perhaps He's calling you to pick up pen and paper, not for others to see but to preserve your own spiritual journey and His messages so that you can be reminded often of His care for you and His guidance to you personally.

I didn't set out to be a writer. I still don't think of myself as an author or professional writer, although God has commissioned me to write this book and one other, *Simply Praying.*[1] I've discovered that God never wastes an experience.

I was a young mother when I started journaling. I was going through a dark period in my life, and I cried out to God for answers. When I quieted my heart to listen, His words to me were so clear that I recorded them. At that time I had not heard of journaling and didn't know anyone who kept a journal. Not long after that dramatic encounter with God, someone I had never met sent my husband a book by her pastor, who was coming to visit us.

The young lady, a new believer in Christ, sent a note saying that she appreciated my husband for befriending her pastor and felt called to pray for her pastor's friends. The gift she sent was *God Calling*.[2]

The book was edited by A. J. Russell, and the contents came from two anonymous Christian ladies, both retired teachers, who were inspired by a book written by Mr. Russell to listen during their prayer times and record God's messages to them. This book inspired me to begin journaling during my prayer times. I started with a spiral notebook and used it as a tool to help me stay focused during my devotions. I wrote requests, listed names of people for whom I was interceding, recorded Scripture promises, and wrote down my thoughts and prayers. Looking back, I appreciate the record my journals provide me of my spiritual journey and progress.

I encourage you to consider journaling. It isn't necessary to worry about grammar, spelling, or punctuation. Don't try to mimic someone else's journaling style. Set your own guidelines. Most organized and compartmentalized journals are not for me. I've tried to be cautious about setting a lot of guidelines in my own journaling, especially rules that constrict me.

Journaling took on a new dimension for me when I started my 10-minute listening times in the summer of 2000. I was prompted to do this by the author of a book I had just finished reading. He suggested giving the first 10 minutes of each day listening to God and writing down His messages. He had been challenged to do this by another writer and told that it was life-changing for him. I was intrigued and wondered if I could listen for 10 whole minutes. From that very first day, I knew my life was headed into new territory with God, and I never dreamed I would witness and participate in so many miracles during my life. I share some of those stories in my book *Simply Praying*.[3]

A friend who is very visual and a lover of nature writes in her private journal stories and allegories that God gives her from His colorful, amazing world. She writes about the story that the stones in the creek bed tell, lessons the intertwining vines exhibit, and songs the babbling brook sings; then she relates these stories to experiences in her own life. She adds scripture and messages God gives her along with stickers, photos of nature, pictures from cards, and sketches she draws. She chooses pretty journals and has found a small, spiral-bound style she prefers.

This friend has a giving heart, and she has supplied many journals for me to give out at prayer retreats. She discovered the value of keeping a journal years ago, not prompted by training and instruction but by visual lessons God impressed on her mind that moved to her heart. She writes with her Bible open and punctuates every page with scripture inserted here and there, along the margins, and between the lines. God has used her writing to do a deep, healing work in her fractured heart.

My friend's way of writing is totally different from mine. I know journalers who use the computer and others who write in expensive leather-bound notebooks. I sat under the teaching of an artist who paints as she listens to God and later adds to her paintings scripture and words God has spoken to her heart.

Jan Johnson tells how she complicated her spiritual progress with a compartmentalized notebook and checklist and invented her own version of "spiritual correctness." She says, "In truth, I needed only one thing—God."[4] She adds, "A journal is a place to talk to God, pour out hurts, to write down questions for God, to sit and enjoy wasting time with Him."[5]

Before or after we pour our hearts out to God, it's safe to listen to what He may have to say. "He doesn't speak to us so we can revel in having a hotline to Him, but to help us in some way: praying for someone more wisely, changing our priorities, intervening in a way previously unclear to us."[6] The list of ways He wants to speak to us and how he wants to intervene in our lives is as varied as the personalities listening to Him. God speaks to each person in his or her own individual way. No two stories are the same.

If you're not keeping a separate notebook for the messages God gives to you as you work through this book, I encourage you to begin one right away. It doesn't have to be a fancy journal, although it can be if that invites you to write. I suggest a loose-leaf or spiral-bound notebook or a journal that's easy to lay flat for writing.

No one has a corner on God; He has messages He wants to give to you. When the Creator of the universe speaks to you, it's important to record what He says. Pick up your pen and paper, and start listening.

Focus for the Month:

Jeremiah 3
Habakkuk
Revelation 1-4

TODAY IS _____

Listen through scripture:

JEREMIAH 36:4-7, NLT:

So Jeremiah sent for Baruch son of Neriah, and as Jeremiah dictated all the prophecies that the LORD had given him, Baruch wrote them on a scroll. Then Jeremiah said to Baruch, "I am a prisoner here and unable to go to the Temple. So you go to the Temple on the next day of fasting, and read the messages from the LORD that I have had you write on this scroll. Read them so the people who are there from all over Judah will hear them. Perhaps even yet they will turn from their evil ways, and ask the LORD's forgiveness before it is too late."

What I sensed God saying to me:

Bring my light to your world. Write about it; tell about it; sing about it. Take each signal seriously. Many are calling, "Send the light." They try to hide their struggles behind clothes, homes, words, fake smiles, jobs, and other barriers. Many a wounded heart is hidden from others. The desperate ones are all around you.

What message is God giving you?

_____

_____

_____

_____

_____

_____

_____

_____

_____

TODAY IS _____

Listen through scripture:

JEREMIAH 36:16-18, NLT:

When they heard all the messages, they looked at one another in alarm. "We must tell the king what we have heard," they said to Baruch. "But first, tell us how you got these messages. Did they come directly from Jeremiah?"

So Baruch explained, "Jeremiah dictated them, and I wrote them down in ink, word for word, on this scroll."

What I sensed God saying to me:

When conflict comes, look to me. When sadness or suffering comes, I will be there. When good times come, I am with you. In your struggles or blessings, I want to be a part of every area of your life, every detail, each decision.

What message is God giving you?

_____

_____

_____

_____

_____

_____

_____

_____

_____

_____

_____

TODAY IS _____

Listen through scripture:

JEREMIAH 36:21-24, NLT:

The king sent Jehudi to get the scroll. Jehudi brought it from Elishama's room and read it to the king as all his officials stood by. It was late autumn, and the king was in a winterized part of the palace, sitting in front of a fire to keep warm. Each time Jehudi finished reading three or four columns, the king took a knife and cut off the section of the scroll. He then threw it into the fire, section by section, until the whole scroll was burned up. Neither the king nor his attendants showed any signs of fear or repentance at what they heard.

What I sensed God saying to me:

Be generous in praise and benevolent to all. I am near. Give everyone a chance. Look for the good in others. If it is not evident, keep that thought to yourself. Use it as a point of prayer, and realize there is a potential for good somewhere in each individual.

What message is God giving you?

_____

_____

_____

_____

_____

_____

_____

_____

_____

_____

TODAY IS _____

Listen through scripture:

JEREMIAH 36:32, NLT:

Jeremiah took another scroll and dictated again to his secretary, Baruch. He wrote everything that had been on the scroll King Jehoiakim had burned in the fire. Only this time he added much more!

What I sensed God saying to me:

Do not let people intimidate you. Take time to listen to their hearts. Do not take on tasks or responsibilities that are not yours to carry. Make sure you do not attribute things to me that are not from me. Yet do not fail to give acknowledgment to me for those gifts and insights that truly do come from me.

What message is God giving you?

_____

_____

_____

_____

_____

_____

_____

_____

_____

_____

_____

_____

_____

TODAY IS _____

Listen through scripture:

JEREMIAH 9:23-24

This is what the LORD says: "Let not the wise man boast of his wisdom or the strong man boast of his strength or the rich man boast of his riches, but let him who boasts boast about this: that he understands and knows me, that I am the LORD, who exercises kindness, justice and righteousness on earth, for in these I delight," declares the LORD.

What I sensed God saying to me:

Do everything without complaining, criticizing, judging unfairly, drawing conclusions before you have all the facts. You cannot change anyone's heart—I can. You can pray. You cannot change your own heart—I can. You can be willing.

What message is God giving you?

_____

_____

_____

_____

_____

_____

_____

_____

_____

_____

TODAY IS _____

Listen through scripture:

JEREMIAH 17:9-10:

> *The heart is deceitful above all things and beyond cure. Who can understand it?*
>
> *I the LORD search the heart and examine the mind, to reward a man according to his conduct, according to what his deeds deserve.*

What I sensed God saying to me:

> *Sit in my presence. Learn from me. Learn from my Word. Hold loosely to the things of this world. All you are doing and experiencing is preparing you for the next world. I know that you cannot fully understand. Live each day as if it could be your last. By this I mean for you to enjoy each day to the fullest and make it count for me.*

What message is God giving you?

_____

_____

_____

_____

_____

_____

_____

_____

_____

_____

_____

TODAY IS _____

Listen through scripture:

HABAKKUK 1:1-4, NLT:

This is the message that the prophet Habakkuk received in a vision. How long, O LORD, must I call for help? But you do not listen! "Violence is everywhere!" I cry, but you do not come to save. Must I forever see these evil deeds? Why must I watch all this misery? Wherever I look, I see destruction and violence. I am surrounded by people who love to argue and fight. The law has become paralyzed, and there is no justice in the courts. The wicked far outnumber the righteous, so that justice has become perverted.

What I sensed God saying to me:

Keep a close watch on your tongue. Let no idle talk come forth from your lips. Conserve your words. Listen more. Listen carefully, intently. Listen with your heart, with my heart. Listen prayerfully with your eyes and emotions. Do the same when you are listening to me. Listen through my Word. Listen through journaling you have done in the past. Listen through music. Be still and hear from me.

What message is God giving you?

_____

_____

_____

_____

_____

_____

_____

_____

TODAY IS _____

Listen through scripture:

HABAKKUK 2:2-4, NLT:

Then the LORD said to me, "Write my answer plainly on tablets, so that a runner can carry the correct message to others. This vision is for future time. It describes the end, and it will be fulfilled. If it seems slow in coming, wait patiently, for it will surely take place. It will not be delayed.

"Look at the proud! They trust in themselves, and their lives are crooked. But the righteous will live by their faithfulness to God."

What I sensed God saying to me:

Your day is in my keeping. Do all for my glory. Do all with a song on your lips. Do all with a glad and joyful heart. Be open to creative thoughts that enter your mind. Love me. Love all that I send your way. Keep in touch with me on all occasions.

What message is God giving you?

_____

_____

_____

_____

_____

_____

_____

_____

_____

_____

TODAY IS _____

Listen through scripture:

HABAKKUK 3:17-19:

Though the fig tree does not bud and there are no grapes on the vines, though the olive crop fails and the fields produce no food, though there are no sheep in the pen and no cattle in the stalls, yet I will rejoice in the LORD. I will be joyful in God my savior.

What I sensed God saying to me:

Realize how much encouragement comes from taking time to write a note or make a phone call. Extend love and blessing to others wherever you go. Do not take any encounter for granted or as chance. Your path crosses the paths of others for a purpose.

What message is God giving you?

_____

_____

_____

_____

_____

_____

_____

_____

_____

_____

_____

_____

TODAY IS _____

Listen through scripture:

REVELATION 2:1-4, NLT:

Write this letter to the angel of the church in Ephesus. . . .

I know the things you do. I have seen your hard work and your patient endurance. I know you don't tolerate evil people. You have examined the claims of those who say they are apostles but are not. You have discovered they are liars. You have patiently suffered for me without quitting.

But I have this complaint against you. You don't love me or each other as you did at first!

What I sensed God saying to me:

Enjoy the beauty of my creation as well as the things I help humanity create. Accept my blessings with a grateful heart. Do not try to earn them nor let your sense of unworthiness rob you of the gifts I give. Receive them with gladness of heart.

What message is God giving you?

_____

_____

_____

_____

_____

_____

_____

_____

_____

_____

TODAY IS _____

Listen through scripture:

REVELATION 2:8-11, NLT:

> *Write this letter to the angel of the church in Smyrna....*
> *I know about your suffering and your poverty—but you are rich! . . .*
> *Don't be afraid of what you are about to suffer. . . . But if you remain faithful*
> *even when facing death, I will give you the crown of life.*

What I sensed God saying to me:

> *You can see that I do not dictate your every minute. I give you choices. I*
> *can help you discern wise choices and will guide you when you ask for specific*
> *advice. I am still waiting for you to follow my call on some past issues. Clear*
> *the clutter. Make time. Take time. Do not be afraid to ask for help. Welcome*
> *my will with gladness!*

What message is God giving you?

_____

_____

_____

_____

_____

_____

_____

_____

_____

_____

TODAY IS _____

Listen through scripture:

REVELATION 2:17, NLT:

Anyone with ears to hear must listen to the Spirit and understand what he is saying to the churches. To everyone who is victorious I will give some of the manna that has been hidden away in heaven. And I will give to each one a white stone, and on the stone will be engraved a new name that no one understands except the one who receives it.

What I sensed God saying to me:

In the hustle and bustle of your day, give me time—time to renew you, time to calm you, time to speak to you. How you use your time will determine your effectiveness.

What message is God giving you?

_____

_____

_____

_____

_____

_____

_____

_____

_____

_____

_____

TODAY IS _____

Listen through scripture:

REVELATION 3:1-5, NLT:

> *Write this letter to the angel of the church in Sardis. . . .*
> *I know all the things you do, and that you have a reputation of being alive—but you are dead. Wake up! Strengthen what little remains, for even what is left is almost dead. I find that your actions do not meet the requirements of my God. Go back to what you heard and believed at first; hold to it firmly. Repent and turn to me again. . . . All who are victorious will be clothed in white. I will never erase their names from the Book of Life, but I will announce before my Father and his angels that they are mine.*

What I sensed God saying to me:

> *The people in your life are far more important than the things you find are hampering your progress. Be ready to let go of things, ideas, and plans that hold you back or bog you down.*

What message is God giving you?

_____

_____

_____

_____

_____

_____

_____

_____

_____

TODAY IS _____

Listen through scripture:

REVELATION 3:7-12:

To the angel of the church in Philadelphia write: These are the words of him who is holy and true, who holds the key of David. What he opens no one can shut, and what he shuts no one can open. I know your deeds. See, I have placed before you an open door that no one can shut. I know that you have little strength, yet you have kept my word and have not denied my name. . . . I am coming soon. Hold on to what you have so that no one will take your crown. Him who overcomes I will make a pillar in the temple of my God. Never again will he leave it. I will write on him the name of my God and the name of the city of my God, the new Jerusalem, which is coming down out of heaven from my God; and I will also write on him my new name.

What I sensed God saying to me:

I am your Elroi, Ishmael, Emmanuel, King of kings, Lord of lords, Redeemer, and Friend. I am your Counselor, Mighty God, Everlasting Father, Savior, Shepherd, Prince of Peace, and your ever-present help in time of trouble. Although you have thousands of things clamoring for your attention, give me this day. Let me speak to you and strengthen you. Keep your heart open and your ears tuned to my calling. Keep your spiritual eyes keen and your thoughts focused on me. This takes discipline.

What message is God giving you?

_____

_____

_____

_____

_____

_____

_____

TODAY IS _____

Listen through scripture:

REVELATION 3:14-21, NLT:

Write this letter to the angel of the church in Laodicea. . . .

I know all the things you do, that you are neither hot nor cold. I wish that you were one or the other! . . . I correct and discipline everyone I love. So be diligent and turn from your indifference.

Look! I stand at the door and knock. If you hear my voice and open the door, I will come in, and we will share a meal together as friends. Those who are victorious will sit with me on my throne, just as I was victorious and sat with my Father on his throne.

What I sensed God saying to me:

I sense your struggles with your self-made rules. Release yourself from bondage, but keep on guard. Many avenues can trip you on your journey. Be quick to respond to my voice. Keep keen spiritual ears so you will be able to discern my voice.

What message is God giving you?

_____

_____

_____

_____

_____

_____

_____

_____

Whether or not you ever write a word that's circulated for others to read, you're a letter from God to others by the life you live. People you don't even know are reading your story daily.

Clearly, you are a letter from Christ showing the result of our ministry among you. This "letter" is written not with pen and ink, but with the Spirit of the living God. It is carved not on tablets of stone, but on human hearts *(2 Corinthians 3:3, NLT)*.

LISTENING AT THE ALTAR

An altar is any sacred place where you meet God. An altar can be in a temple or church building or outdoors, in our homes, at the kitchen table, in a closet, or beside a lake—anywhere we bow in obedience before God.

The altar is a place for confession and forgiveness. At the altar Isaiah's lips were touched by burning coals, and he was told that his guilt had been taken away and his sins atoned for. God then sent Isaiah to deliver a hard message that the people were not willing to accept. (See Isaiah 1:1-6.)

Altars are places where we come in obedience to God. In 1 Kings we find the exciting story of Elijah when he was told by God to go to King Ahab and tell him that God was sending rain soon although the famine was still severe. Elijah risked his life and obeyed by challenging the 450 prophets of Baal to a contest. They shouted, cut themselves, and raved from morning until evening with no response. Then Elijah repaired the altar of the Lord, piled on wood, added the sacrifice, and drenched the offering and wood with water three times. (See 1 Kings 18:36-39.)

Altars are also places of remembrance. The Lord told Moses, "Build my altar wherever I cause my name to be remembered, and I will come to you and bless you" (Exodus 20:24, NLT).

Jesus spoke of the altar and said, "So if you are presenting a sacrifice at the altar in the Temple and you suddenly remember that someone has something against you, leave your sacrifice there at the altar. Go and be reconciled to that person. Then come and offer your sacrifice to God" (Matthew 5:23-24, NLT).

● ● ● ● ● ●

The first time I remember kneeling at the altar at church was during Vacation Bible School the summer between my second- and third-grade years. The leader had invited those of us who wanted to ask Jesus into our hearts to come to the altar to pray. My cousin was crying and went forward along with almost all the other boys and girls. Although I was saying to myself that I already loved Jesus, I followed the crowd, not really understanding why I was there.

Later that summer my family moved to another town, and my cousin and aunt came to visit. Our new church was having a revival. One night before the service, while my cousin and I were waiting to go to church with the family, she asked if I would like to go with her to the altar to be saved. I was seven and did not know I needed to be "saved." She explained to me that she had watched people give testimonies after kneeling at the altar, and she had prepared hers. Then she offered to help me plan one. We memorized and practiced on each other. It took three nights before we got the courage to go. Once I got to the altar, I began weeping but did not totally understand it all. My cousin cried throughout her testimony and forgot hers. I recited mine proudly and perfectly.

The next day she and I had a big fuss, and I thought, *It didn't work.* My heart remained tender toward God through the years. I often sat on the front row at church and found myself at the altar many times at the close of a service when an altar call was given. I could usually think of something I needed to confess—sassing my mother, arguing with my sister, throwing a temper tantrum.

A few years later I stood at the altar to join the church and, after college, to say my marriage vows. When I was keenly aware of selfishness in my marriage, I made an altar of my apartment sofa one night. I was desperately seeking a deeper relationship with God and was remorsefully aware of my self-centeredness, bad attitudes, temper, pride; I was in great need of God's help. I stayed there until sunrise, pouring out my heart to God, relinquishing self, and allowing Him to cleanse and fill me with His Spirit. A short time later I was introduced to the book *Hinds' Feet on High Places,* by Hannah Hurnard.

In this allegory about a young maiden named Much Afraid, the Chief Shepherd invited her—crippled, with a crooked mouth, and true to her name—to journey from the Valley of Humiliation to the High Places in His Kingdom. She had been in the service of the Chief Shepherd for some time and longed to go the mountains she could see in the distance. She was very excited when the invitation came to leave the valley and her fearing relatives to travel to the high places but was very confused when early in the journey the Chief Shepherd gave her Sorrow and Suffering to be her traveling companions and guides.[1]

Many times along the journey as she faced detours and directions from the Chief Shepherd that she could not understand, she had to build an altar and lay down her trembling self-will. When the road led down into the wilderness seemingly away from the mountains, she built her first altar, and as she laid her trembling self-will on the altar, a spurt of fire came and consumed it. In the ashes she saw a dark-colored little stone. "Pick it up and take it with you," the Chief Shepherd said gently. "It is a memorial of the altar which you built."[2]

There were numerous altars to build and stones to collect along the journey. In the desert, on the Shores of Loneliness, at her impatience with the Chief Shepherd when her enemies Pride and Self-Pity were lurking, through the woods and valleys, she built altars and placed her self-will there. She continued beyond the Forest of Danger and Tribulation through floods and storms to the Valley of Loss and the grave on the mountain. There He asked her if she could trust Him completely even though it seemed He had deceived her. During the great storm she fingered all the stones of remembrance she had collected and realized she could not part with any of His promises. She then picked up a stone to add to the others and said, "Though He slay me, YET WILL I TRUST IN HIM" (Job 13:15).[3]

When she awakened from the grave on the side of the mountain after offering her final sacrifice of self, she discovered that she now had hinds' feet and could jump and leap around on the mountains with the Chief Shepherd, exploring new heights and learning beautiful lessons from Him. Her name was changed to Grace and Glory, and she learned that she had been chosen as the traveling companion for Sorrow and Suffering, whose names had been changed to Joy and Peace.[4]

Where is the Chief Shepherd calling you on your journey as you cringe and resist going? What altars of confession or obedience do you need to build? Are you trying to live the Christian life in your own crippled, much-afraid state?

• • • • • •

I have had many more altars to build after that all-night surrender. When we moved to a church that had a music program that did not measure up to that of our previous church, I wondered how I would survive it. God spoke clearly to me and said, *You did not come here to worship the mu-*

sic—or the people or the sermon or the style of worship; you came to worship me and me alone. At open-altar time during the pastoral prayer, I knelt, crying out to God, placing my trembling self-will on the altar.

At a living room chair altar, I took my daughter to the Cross and placed her at the feet of Jesus when I feared she might be making some unwise choices while away at college. I reminded God that I had dedicated her to Him as an infant and that she was still His. When she graduated from college and decided to stay in another city to work and live alone, I knelt beside her bed, relinquishing control. At that bedside altar, God reminded me that I was no longer her parent. As her mother, I was still to love and pray for her, but she was now an adult older than I was when I married and started teaching school.

My most recent altar was built here in my office where I am writing this book. I have a little bench where I have placed the notebook containing the unfinished manuscript of *Simply Listening*. I kneel there daily to once again give it to God and seek His help in completing the book He asked me to write.

Whether your altar is in an open field, on a church pew, beside your bathtub, or at any location you find yourself meeting God, you'll leave the altar changed if you place your trembling self-will there and wait for God to speak His wisdom to you.

● ● ● ● ● ●

Find a sacred place often this month to meet with God.

Lay down bitterness, pride, anger, envy, gossip, control, self-will.

Confess sin, an unforgiving attitude, doubt, lack of faith, disobedience.

Accept forgiveness, faith, peace, joy, God's blessings.

Renew vows, commitments, covenants with God.

Remember times He has met you in the past and His promises to you.

Allow Him to cleanse, purify, sanctify, and make you holy.

Remain at the altar listening for His message to you, and collect a memorial stone to take with you.

Why don't you lay your burden at the altar and go free?

Focus for the Month:

1 Samuel 7

1 Kings 8; 9:1

2 Chronicles 6-7
Romans 8 and 12
1 Corinthians 13
1 Peter 1
2 Peter 1

TODAY IS _____

Listen through scripture:

GENESIS 12:7:

> The LORD appeared to Abram and said, "To your offspring I will give this land." So he built an altar there to the LORD, who appeared to him.

What I sensed God saying to me:

I have made my home in your heart. You have given me control of every part. At times I illuminate new corners, shelves, and storage areas to give you insight. Your mind can be controlled by filling it with scripture and focusing on me. Reading and singing scripture and looking to me will transform your thoughts. Take me with you to every event; do not leave me out of any activity of your life. Place your talents and gifts in my hands, your weaknesses too. Although you have given me ownership of your heart and life, I also want to help you with housekeeping. You have learned that it's a job too big for you to handle alone.

What message is God giving you?

_____

_____

_____

_____

_____

_____

_____

_____

_____

_____

TODAY IS _____

Listen through scripture:

GENESIS 35:1-3:

Then God said to Jacob, "Go up to Bethel and settle there, and build an altar there to God, who appeared to you when you were fleeing from your brother Esau. So Jacob said to his household and to those who were with him, "Get rid of the foreign gods you have with you, and purify yourselves and change your clothes. Then come let us go up to Bethel, where I will build an altar to God, who answered me in the day of my distress and who has been with me wherever I have gone."

What I sensed God saying to me:

Do not recoil from the things I ask you to do that may make you uncomfortable. Do not be afraid; I the Lord, your God, will walk before you.

What message is God giving you?

_____

_____

_____

_____

_____

_____

_____

_____

_____

_____

_____

TODAY IS _____

Listen through scripture:

DEUTERONOMY 27:1-8:

Moses and the elders of Israel commanded the people: "Keep all these commands that I give you today. When you have crossed the Jordan into the land the LORD your God is giving you, set up some large stones. . . . Write on them all the words of this law . . . and when you have crossed the Jordan . . . build there an altar . . . and offer burnt offerings on it to the LORD your God. Sacrifice fellowship offerings there, eating them and rejoicing in the presence of the LORD your God. And you shall write very clearly all the words of this law on these stones you have set up."

What I sensed God saying to me:

Do not allow the enemy to feed your mind doubtful thoughts. Counter those thoughts with praise, Scripture promises, songs, and examples of my work in the past. I came to bring freedom, not bondage; truth, not doubt; peace, not war. Yet you are in a battle with evil. Victory is assured. The struggles, however, will be real. Use the weapons I have given, which include repentance, binding yourself to me, pronouncing my decrees, claiming my promises, shouting the victory.

What message is God giving you?

_____

_____

_____

_____

_____

_____

_____

_____

TODAY IS _____

Listen through scripture:

JOSHUA 8:30:

    *Joshua built on Mount Ebal an altar to the L*ORD*, the God of Israel, as Moses the servant of the L*ORD *had commanded the Israelites. He built it according to what is written in the Book of the Law of Moses—an altar of uncut stones, on which no iron tool had been used. On it they offered to the L*ORD *burnt offerings and sacrificed fellowship offerings. There, in the presence of the Israelites, Joshua copied on stones the law of Moses, which he had written.*

What I sensed God saying to me:

    Yes, your world is in a mess. Sin is ugly. And it's true that freedom isn't free. It never has been. Your freedom from sin came at a great price. There will be no end of struggle until heaven. That gives you all the more reason to look forward to it and to rejoice when one of my children comes to be with me. I know it does not make sense to the unchristian world. It should be clear to you, though, because it affects the way you grieve and view life and death.

What message is God giving you?

_____

_____

_____

_____

_____

_____

_____

_____

_____

_____

TODAY IS _____

Listen through scripture:

I SAMUEL 7:15-17:

Samuel continued as judge over Israel all the days of his life. . . . But he always went back to Ramah, where his home was . . . and he built an altar there to the LORD.

What I sensed God saying to me:

Although a war is raging in your world, I have not lost control. I have always been in the business of working good in spite of evil. I realize you have puzzled over the good and evil issue for years. You will never be able to fully sort it all out. Your faith has been bolstered and established in spite of questioning and inner struggles. Your years of walking with me have taught you lessons that could be learned only in my school of knowledge.

What message is God giving you?

_____

_____

_____

_____

_____

_____

_____

_____

_____

_____

_____

TODAY IS _____

Listen through scripture:

2 CHRONICLES 4:19 AND 5:13-14:

Solomon also made all the furnishings that were in God's temple: the golden altar; the tablets on which was the bread of the Presence (4:19).

Then the temple of the LORD was filled with a cloud, and the priests could not perform their service because of the cloud, for the glory of the LORD filled the temple of God (5:13-14).

What I sensed God saying to me:

Listen for my whispers. I am the song of your heart, the joy of your song. I, the Lord your God, will walk before you, preparing the way, clearing the path. Keep your eyes on the goal, which is to look always to me, to do my will. The shadows may hide my face momentarily. Keep moving in the direction I have last pointed out to you.

What message is God giving you?

_____

_____

_____

_____

_____

_____

_____

_____

_____

_____

TODAY IS _____

Listen through scripture:

2 CHRONICLES 7:11-14, NLT:

So Solomon finished the Temple of the LORD, as well as the royal palace. He completed everything he had planned to do in the construction of the Temple and the palace. Then one night the LORD appeared to Solomon and said,

"I have heard your prayer and have chosen this Temple as the place for making sacrifices. At times I might shut up the heavens so that no rain falls, or command grasshoppers to devour your crops, or send plagues among you. Then if my people who are called by my name will humble themselves and pray and seek my face and turn from their wicked ways, I will hear from heaven and will forgive their sins and restore their land."

What I sensed God saying to me:

Be still and inhale my Spirit, wait in my presence, and bask in the beauty of my creation. Quiet yourself before me often throughout the day. I will give you eyes to see the invisible, ears to hear the inaudible, a mind to see the inconceivable.

What message is God giving you?

_____

_____

_____

_____

_____

_____

_____

_____

_____

TODAY IS _____

Listen through scripture:

MATTHEW 3:11:

I baptize you with water for repentance. But after me will come one who is more powerful than I, whose sandals I am unfit to carry. He will baptize you with the Holy Spirit and with fire.

What I sensed God saying to me:

You really do not have to beg me for the salvation of souls. I understand the thought of urgency and passion behind the word "beg," but I delight to bring salvation to anyone willing to receive. Maybe the better approach is to beg that you will be willing to be used as an instrument in spreading the good news of salvation. Be on the lookout for hungry souls; they are hiding all around you.

What message is God giving you?

_____

_____

_____

_____

_____

_____

_____

_____

_____

_____

TODAY IS _____

Listen through scripture:

ROMANS 12:1-2

I urge you, brothers, in view of God's mercy, to offer your bodies as living sacrifices, holy and pleasing to God—this is your spiritual act of worship. Do not conform any longer to the pattern of this world, but be transformed by the renewing of your mind. Then you will be able to test and approve what God's will is—his good, pleasing and perfect will.

What I sensed God saying to me:

I am revealing areas of your life that I want to enter. You have asked me to expose anything in your heart that needs to be cleansed, removed, forgiven, or relinquished. I am shining my light in the dark corners and illuminating your heart so that you can see these things. My purpose is not to make you feel remorseful, although you will. I want you to turn these things over to me. Humility will come as a result. Just your acknowledgment of the need to let go of these things is the beginning of change.

What message is God giving you?

_____

_____

_____

_____

_____

_____

_____

_____

TODAY IS _____

Listen through scripture:

I THESSALONIANS 5:23-24:

May God himself, the God of peace, sanctify you through and through. May your whole spirit, soul and body be kept blameless at the coming of our Lord Jesus Christ. The one who calls you is faithful and he will do it.

What I sensed God saying to me:

The way is marked, sometimes clearly; sometimes the signs are obscured. Your busyness, your finite mind, your experiences cause you to miss my road markers at times. Your doubts and lack of faith may make my directions seem impossible. The way will become clearer as you release your doubts to me and give me your faith—small as it may seem. Spend time with me, and allow me to interpret past experiences and enlighten your mind and the spiritual eyes of your heart.

What message is God giving you?

_____

_____

_____

_____

_____

_____

_____

_____

_____

_____

_____

TODAY IS _____

Listen through scripture:

I JOHN 3:2-3

Dear friends, now we are children of God, and what we will be has not yet been made known. But we know that when he appears, we shall be like him, for we shall see him as he is. Everyone who has this hope in him purified himself, just as he is pure.

What I sensed God saying to me:

Do not align yourself with the ungodly. Tear down every idol in your life. Legalism and being judgmental are both dire states for a man or woman to endure, bondage that robs one of joy and gladness. Visages of these attitudes lurk everywhere. They're easier to detect in others than in oneself.

What message is God giving you?

_____

_____

_____

_____

_____

_____

_____

_____

_____

_____

_____

TODAY IS _____

Listen through scripture:

I CORINTHIANS 13:1-3, NLT:

If I could speak all the languages of earth and of angels, but didn't love others, I would only be a noisy gong or a clanging cymbal. If I had the gift of prophecy, and if I understood all of God's secret plans and possessed all knowledge, and if I had such faith that I could move mountains, but didn't love others, I would be nothing. If I gave everything I have to the poor and even sacrificed my body, I could boast about it, but if I didn't love others, I would have gained nothing.

What I sensed God saying to me:

Friendship is the key. Your task is to befriend and teach others to befriend.

What message is God giving you?

_____

_____

_____

_____

_____

_____

_____

_____

_____

_____

TODAY IS _____

Listen through scripture:

I CORINTHIANS 13:7, NLT:

Love never gives up, never loses faith, is always hopeful, and endures through every circumstance.

What I sensed God saying to me:

I will reveal specific individuals to you and ways to pray. More of my time was given to a small group of people; yes, I touched the masses but devoted extended time with my disciples and a few followers. You cannot give large blocks of time to everyone. Like the woman at the well, I will send some people into your life for a brief but focused encounter. Others will be in your life for an extended time for deeper, personal, and spiritual mentoring.

What message is God giving you?

_____

_____

_____

_____

_____

_____

_____

_____

_____

_____

_____

TODAY IS _____

Listen through scripture:

2 PETER 1:3-4, NLT:

By his divine power, God has given us everything we need for living a godly life. We have received all of this by coming to know him, the one who called us to himself by means of his marvelous glory and excellence. And because of his glory and excellence, he has given us great and precious promises. These are the promises that enable you to share his divine nature and escape the world's corruption caused by human desires.

What I sensed God saying to me:

A daily walk with me and your prayers are essential for a pure and holy heart to the end, for a free and joyful spirit, for a life of godly influence, for a peaceful heart. I am here with love and grace to guide you. Sense my presence. Remember this holy place, this divine moment.

What message is God giving you?

_____

_____

_____

_____

_____

_____

_____

_____

_____

_____

TODAY IS _____

Listen through scripture:

2 PETER 1:5-11, NLT:

Make every effort to respond to God's promises. Supplement your faith with a generous provision of moral excellence, and moral excellence with knowledge, and knowledge with self-control, and self-control with patient endurance, and patient endurance with godliness, and godliness with brotherly affection, and brotherly affection with love for everyone. The more you grow like this, the more productive and useful you will be in your knowledge of our Lord Jesus Christ. . . . Do these things, and you will never fall away. Then God will give you a grand entrance into the eternal kingdom of our Lord and Savior Jesus Christ.

What I sensed God saying to me:

Your life is getting ready to make a big turn. Anticipate it, but do not try to predict what it is. Prepare yourself in the ways I prompt you.

What message is God giving you?

_____

_____

_____

_____

_____

_____

_____

_____

_____

_____

One day as Much Afraid, now named Grace and Glory, and her companions looked over the edge of the High Places, she looked down into the Low Places far below and recognized that she was looking into the Valley of Humiliation. Her heart throbbed with pain. Tears flowed, and she discovered that her feelings had dramatically changed toward her miserable relatives who lived there. She now realized that they were tormented beings, slaves to sin and their horrible natures. They began to discuss how they could go down and persuade the people to follow the Shepherd. "Then Peace who before had been Suffering said quietly, 'I have noticed that when people are brought into sorrow and suffering, or loss, or humiliation, or grief, or into some place of great need, they sometimes become ready to know the Shepherd and to seek His help.'"[5]

Think about that as you listen in the dark times.

LISTENING IN THE DARK TIMES

Jacob's much-loved son Joseph was sold by his brothers to traveling Ishmaelite traders; lied about by Potiphar's wife, resulting in imprisonment; forgotten by the cupbearer when he was released after Joseph interpreted his dream. He was undeservedly punished repeatedly. Yet, he was able to one day say to his brothers, "You intended to harm me, but God intended it all for good. He brought me to this position so I could save the lives of many people" (Genesis 50:20, NLT).

While captives in Babylon, Shadrach, Meshach, and Abednego faced the fiery furnace after refusing to bow down to worship foreign gods and King Nebuchadnezzar's gold statue. Before being thrown into the fire, they announced, "If we are thrown into the blazing furnace, the God whom we serve is able to save us. He will rescue us from your power, Your Majesty. But even if he doesn't, we want to make it clear to you, Your Majesty, that we will never serve your gods or worship the gold statue you have set up" (Daniel 3:17-18, NLT).

The flames were so hot that the soldiers who threw them in were killed, yet, Shadrach, Meshach, and Abednego came forth without a hair singed or clothing scorched. When the king looked into the fire, he saw four men, not three, walking around in the fire. This resulted in King Nebuchadnezzar's praising God and elevating the three Hebrew young men to higher positions in the province of Babylon. (See Daniel 3:19-25.)

God uses strange situations to fulfill His purposes.

• • • • • •

I was privileged to hear Dorie Van Stone speak at a women's conference I attended. Dorie told that, as an unloved and battered child, she became incorrigible. One day some university students came to her orphanage for a religious service. Since Dorie had no idea of what to expect, and none of the boys and girls seemed able to explain to her what a religious service was, she chose to sit in the back.

When the prettiest girl in the group stood to begin the service, her first words were "God loves you." Dorie shouted from the back row, "He does not!" However, she listened to the testimonies of these lovely young ladies.

At the close of the assembly, as they were leaving, the first speaker turned and said again, "I want you to remember that God loves you." No one had ever told Dorie that she was loved. Rather, she had been verbally and physically abused by caregivers. When Dorie fell into bed that night, she told God that if He loved her, she wanted to be His girl. For a short time a Christian matron came to the orphanage, and as Dorie left to go to a foster home, the matron thrust a small New Testament into Dorie's hands. It was the first gift Dorie had ever received.

Although the abuse continued and worsened at her new home, Dorie clung to the promises she read in the New Testament.[1] In spite of abominable circumstances, Dorie became an artist, author, missionary, pastor's wife, mother, and an internationally known speaker. Her story is truly incredible, and she displays God's amazing grace. She heard God speak to her heart in the darkest of days, and His love and promises sustained her.

• • • • • •

I was loved by my parents and extended family, my husband and in-laws, my friends and church associates, but no one knew how unlovely and unlovable I felt. I was the mother of two preschoolers, had gone through two difficult pregnancies, and was physically depleted and desperate. My youngest child, a toddler at the time, required less sleep than I did. She was energetic, quick, and everywhere at once! Lanissa sometimes darted outside as I opened the door to reach for the mail. She ran so fast that I had to chase her across the street and through unfenced yards several homes away to catch her.

My husband's office was in an office building near property owned by the church he pastored. He left in our only car early in the morning and stayed at the office late, overseeing the church building project. Sometimes he didn't get home until the children and I had gone to bed.

Housebound with two children, not well, and facing dark times, I was so weak that I could hardly lift my arm to get a cup from the kitchen cabinet. My husband was so concerned that he finally told me that if I did not make an appointment with the doctor, he would. Medical tests showed chemical imbalances that included low thyroid function and low blood sugar. The doctor started me on medication but warned that he expected it to be several months before I would be well.

One day after an emotional outburst, I told Curtis, "I'm not praying anymore. Prayer doesn't work." I had called out to God many times for healing. It wasn't happening—at least not quickly enough for me. I decided to give God the silent treatment I thought He deserved.

I'm not sure at what point I began talking with Him again, but because He had been a part of my life so long, I missed communicating with Him. I later learned that I had misinterpreted His silence. Joseph Bentz says, "Nothing is as easy to misinterpret as silence. If you don't believe that, take a few minutes to think of some times when someone has misinterpreted your own silence. Have you ever been accused of pouting or being angry when in fact you were merely deep in thought or tired? . . . Has someone ever interpreted your silence as disapproval when it really meant satisfaction or shyness?"[2] He continues, "As Christians, even when we are practicing the kinds of spiritual disciplines like solitude and prayer . . . most of us will experience times in our lives when God goes silent. For reasons unknown to us, we feel the pain of the withdrawal of His presence. Tragically, we may misinterpret God's silence and give up on Him altogether."[3]

This is where I found myself, but I also learned that it doesn't have to happen. Joseph Benz says, "As strange as it may sound, God may be doing some of His most significant spiritual work in us during those dry times."[4]

My son, Kevin, was six years old and in school. I was slowly improving, but Curtis decided to put Lanissa and me onto a plane and send us to stay with my parents so they could care for Lanissa while I rested. On the way to the airport, I told Curtis that all I wanted to be was a good wife, mother, and pastor's wife, and I felt I was a failure in all roles. He responded by saying that maybe I had an unreachable ideal greater than God's. I thought about that on the flight to Tennessee.

After I arrived at my parents' home, I stayed in bed all day for more than a week, and they cared for Lanissa. I came out of my room only at mealtimes. Prompted by Curtis's remark on the way to the airport, I began to realize that I had been telling God how to fix me and had never listened once to what He might have to say to me. One day I knelt beside the bed and told God I was going to stay there all day—and all night if necessary—until I heard from Him. After kneeling momentarily, I found a pen and paper to write down what He told me.

God began to reveal truth to me. He told me many things I had needed to know about expectations I put on myself and expectations I allowed others to put on me. He told me that if I took time to listen to Him, I would learn to please Him alone, and He would free me from insecurities and my need for the approval of others. I still have those notes from God.

With the Holy Spirit as my counselor, I went back in my memory to my early childhood and took a prayer walk through my life. I relived happy times, and I allowed God to bring healing for troubling events. When I came to a change point in my life involving a hurt, a rejection, a broken relationship, I allowed God to help me work through it. I asked Him to reveal to me through His Holy Spirit things He felt I should know, such as wrong motives, bad attitudes, and denial of the real issues.[5] I asked forgiveness and granted forgiveness, moving step by step through my life. I confessed and asked the Lord to forgive me of all the ugly things I saw. I allowed Him to forgive through me persons who had brought hurt into my life both intentionally and unintentionally.[6]

Eventually I reached the present and knew I was free. I called Curtis and said, "I'm a free woman!"

That was not the last dark period; there have been others. We have faced cloudy, uncertain days, illnesses, and family crises. No doubt, dark days will come again in the future. We live in a fallen world, and God sends rain on both the righteous and unrighteous. (See Matthew 5:45.) However, His promises hold me steady.

I eventually wrote a life mission statement: "To encourage discovery and enlighten hearts as I leave behind a legacy of hope to those God places in my life." Hope! Yes, there is hope—living hope—and treasures to be found, even when we're in dark places!

• • • • • •

Turn to God's Word for comfort and strength for yourself and others when dark times come. This month's Scripture passages have been selected to bring you light and hope.

Focus for the Month:

Isaiah 45
Daniel 1-3
Psalms 62, 86, 116, 118, 130

TODAY IS _____

Listen through scripture:

ISAIAH 45:9, NLT:

What sorrow awaits those who argue with their Creator. Does a clay pot argue with its maker? Does the clay dispute with the one who shapes it, saying, "Stop, you're doing it wrong!" Does the pot exclaim, "How clumsy can you be?"

What I sensed God saying to me:

Yes, I came to bind up the broken hearts of my children and to heal their wounds and bring comfort to their souls. You are a part of that plan. Remember that you are to help carry the burdens of those I send your way; however, you are to bring those burdens to me, for I am the divine burden-bearer. Grieving is a part of the healing. I'm giving you this season of time when your personal burdens are not as heavy so that you can help carry the weight of others' loads.

What message is God giving you?

_____

_____

_____

_____

_____

_____

_____

_____

_____

_____

TODAY IS _____

Listen through scripture:

ISAIAH 45:10-12, NLT:

How terrible it would be if a newborn baby said to its father, "Why was I born?" Or if it said to its mother, "Why did you make me this way?"

This is what the LORD says—the Holy One of Israel and your Creator. "Do you question what I do for my children? Do you give me orders about the work of my hands? I am the one who made the earth and created people to live on it. With my hands I stretched out the heavens. All the stars are at my command."

What I sensed God saying to me:

Many times a day my angels are watching over you, protecting you—more times than you can imagine. I allowed you to see it clearly today. Give me your grief for imperfections. You have grieved enough. You are free. I can make use of every experience, every circumstance. Leave it all at the foot of the Cross.

What message is God giving you?

_____

_____

_____

_____

_____

_____

_____

_____

_____

_____

TODAY IS _____

Listen through scripture:

ISAIAH 45:18, NLT:

> For the LORD is God, and he created the heavens and earth and put everything in place. He made the world to be lived in, not to be a place of empty chaos. "I am the LORD," he says, "and there is no other."

What I sensed God saying to me:

> You are wrestling with some big issues. Your finite mind is trying to sort through the incomprehensible. Take the truth you do comprehend and allow that truth to work in your life. You use appliances and technological resources every day without understanding how they work. Accept that it is the same in the Spirit world. Use your understanding of this scripture to operate in your life. Keep moving forward, undaunted by the forces of doubt.

What message is God giving you?

_____

_____

_____

_____

_____

_____

_____

_____

_____

_____

_____

TODAY IS _____

Listen through scripture:

ISAIAH 45:24, NLT:

The people will declare, "The LORD is the source of all my righteousness and strength."

What I sensed God saying to me:

You have struggled with an issue yesterday and today. You have grieved and begged for my counsel, and I have responded. Allow yourself to grieve, to weep, to mourn, but realize that you have warned others, and they have the freedom to make their own choices. You are hurt, and you feel your warnings have gone unheeded. The enemy is subtle in his tactics; he is a deceiver. Your task is to love and pray. My heart grieves also when I give my word and warning to my loved ones, and they won't hear it. I share your sadness. Continue to do spiritual battle on behalf of those for whom you are concerned.

What message is God giving you?

_____

_____

_____

_____

_____

_____

_____

_____

_____

_____

_____

TODAY IS _____

Listen through scripture:

ISAIAH 40:13-14, NLT

Who is able to advise the Spirit of the LORD? Who knows enough to give him advice or teach him? Has the LORD ever needed anyone's advice? Does he need instruction about what is good? Did someone teach him what is right or show him the path of justice?

What I sensed God saying to me:

Cover your whole life with your prayers: your home, your family, your office, your schedule, your errands, your tasks. Take each step cautiously, not with fear and trembling but with prayerful care. You are about to step into a small valley, yet I am with you. Do not forget that important fact. I know you do not want to hear those words, but I will remind you that it is all for my glory. Read these words often, for you will not see these things immediately. Over time you will look back on the ways I have led and worked. I realize this puzzles you now. Allow me to cover you with my Spirit. Consecrate yourself anew.

What message is God giving you?

_____

_____

_____

_____

_____

_____

_____

_____

_____

_____

TODAY IS _____

Listen through scripture:

ISAIAH 42:5-7:

This is what God the LORD says—he who created the heavens and stretched them out, who spread out the earth and all that comes out of it, who gives breath to its people, and life to those who walk on it: "I, the LORD, have called you in righteousness; I will take hold of your hand. I will keep you and will make you to be a covenant for the people and a light for the Gentiles, to open eyes that are blind, to free captives from prison and to release from the dungeon those who sit in darkness."

What I sensed God saying to me:

I am calling you to grieve for the sins of your family and friends. I realize that this is a heavy assignment. Just remember that I took on the sins of the world on the Cross and agonized over that assignment at Gethsemane. Greater is your God than the enemy who is trying to rule the world. The battle is getting more intense. Think of yourself as a warrior against evil. I am the commander of your army.

What message is God giving you?

_____

_____

_____

_____

_____

_____

_____

_____

TODAY IS _____

Listen through scripture:

ISAIAH 42:8-9:

> *I am the* LORD; *that is my name! I will not give my glory to another or my praise to idols. See, the former things have taken place, and new things I declare; before they spring into being I announce them to you.*

What I sensed God saying to me:

> *Put on my armor, take up my Word, and pray to stand against the evil one. He is the defeated one, but he has not accepted that fact. I am your defender, but the fight will be hard and long. You wonder why the journey to wholeness is so rough and seems to have no end. Would you desire any other way but my way? You have made the choice to travel with me; you must make that choice daily. Travel on. Travel light. Keep your roadmap and light in your hand.*

What message is God giving you?

_____

_____

_____

_____

_____

_____

_____

_____

_____

_____

_____

TODAY IS _____

Listen through scripture:

ISAIAH 43:2-3, NLT:

When you go through deep waters, I will be with you. When you go through rivers of difficulty, you will not drown. When you walk through the fire of oppression, you will not be burned up; the flames will not consume you. For I am the LORD your God, the Holy One of Israel, your Savior.

What I sensed God saying to me:

Not all of life is glamorous. Not all vacations are fantasyland, devoid of reality. The incident you observed today will be a picture in your mind for days to come to remind you to grieve the plight of the abused and oppressed. You have grief work to do. I will give you the time, place, and strength.

What message is God giving you?

_____

_____

_____

_____

_____

_____

_____

_____

_____

_____

_____

_____

TODAY IS _____

Listen through scripture:

ISAIAH 61:3, NLT:

To all who mourn in Israel, he will give a crown of beauty for ashes, joyous blessing instead of mourning, festive praise instead of despair. In their righteousness, they will be like great oaks that the LORD has planted for his own glory.

What I sensed God saying to me:

I see your grief over past sins and failures. You realize that your remorse will not change the past or redeem it. Godly sorrow is a step in the repentance process, but I must remind you that you are telling me again and again about past failures that have been forgiven and are totally under the blood, buried in the depths of the sea and never to be remembered against you. Give them back to me and leave them there. I alone can redeem the past. The work is done. Claim victory.

What message is God giving you?

_____

_____

_____

_____

_____

_____

_____

_____

_____

TODAY IS _____

Listen through scripture:

ISAIAH 64:8:

Yet, O LORD, you are our Father. We are the clay, you are the potter; we are all the work of your hand.

What I sensed God saying to me:

Your heart is heavy because of news that grieves you but doesn't surprise you. You have brought it to me; I will help you walk through this. You are puzzled that I didn't give you specific warnings of impending doom; however, I have given you insights bit by bit. You know that anyone who does not give me total control is capable of any evil. You have the tools to deal with these issues. I did not say that the road will be easy. You cannot fix or control every situation. Many others have lived through similar heartaches. I know the pain is real, but I have been preparing and equipping you for this battle. You will stand. You will not crumble.

What message is God giving you?

_____

_____

_____

_____

_____

_____

_____

_____

_____

_____

TODAY IS _____

Listen through scripture:

PSALM 36:5-7, NLT:

Your unfailing love, O LORD, is as vast as the heavens; your faithfulness reaches beyond the clouds. Your righteousness is like the mighty mountains, your justice like the ocean depths. You care for people and animals alike, O LORD. How precious is your unfailing love, O God! All humanity finds shelter in the shadow of your wings.

What I sensed God saying to me:

The sting of words spoken that you never wanted to hear could easily cause you to withdraw or distance yourself. Face it honestly. If there are no actions or responses that will benefit the relationship, let the words and attitudes go; allow them to ascend to me. Do not pick up past experiences or heap guilt upon yourself in any way. Walk forward, knowing that I am with you even in the unexpected. I am your deliverer.

What message is God giving you?

_____

_____

_____

_____

_____

_____

_____

_____

_____

TODAY IS _____

Listen through scripture:

PSALM 62:5-8, NLT:

Let all that I am wait quietly before God, for my hope is in him. He alone is my rock and my salvation, my fortress where I will not be shaken. My victory and honor come from God alone. He is my refuge, a rock where no enemy can reach me. O my people, trust in him at all times. Pour out your heart to him, for God is our refuge.

What I sensed God saying to me:

Every person lives in a hidden world of his or her own, even those who reveal the most about themselves. You are curious about the unrevealed corners of the hearts and emotions of those near and dear to you. You will never see and know all. You could not bear it; yet I sometimes give you discernment beyond the visible. This is not to crush you but to enlighten you as you pray and relate to others.

What message is God giving you?

_____

_____

_____

_____

_____

_____

_____

_____

_____

TODAY IS _____

Listen through scripture:

PSALM 86:1, NLT:

> *Bend down, O LORD, and hear my prayer; answer me, for I need your help.*

What I sensed God saying to me:

Sometimes you learn more about an individual or situation than you want to know, and I allow you to become aware of things that are troubling. Many of the stories you hear from others are filled with degradation. My grace can reach even these dark places. Watch me work. I have given you spiritual discernment; many do not choose to cultivate their discernment. Never use your insight to tear down or cause despair. I am the hope-giver, and sometimes I use you to join me in extending hope.

What message is God giving you?

_____

_____

_____

_____

_____

_____

_____

_____

_____

_____

TODAY IS _____

Listen through scripture:

PSALM 116:12-14, NLT:

What can I offer the LORD for all he has done for me? I will lift up the cup of salvation and praise the LORD's name for saving me. I will keep my promises to the LORD in the presence of all his people.

What I sensed God saying to me:

It is true that I am an untamable God. Do not try to fit me into a box or mold that humanity has made. Do not skip over troubling scripture. Suffering teaches lessons that could not otherwise be learned. Can you say with James, "I am a slave of God and the Master Jesus"? "Consider it a sheer gift when tests and challenges come to you from all sides. You know that under pressure your faith-life shows its true colors." I do not want you to be deficient in any way. "Ask boldly, believingly, without a second thought" (James 1:6, TM).

What message is God giving you?

_____

_____

_____

_____

_____

_____

_____

_____

_____

_____

_____

TODAY IS _____

Listen through scripture:

JEREMIAH 33:1-3:

While Jeremiah was still confined in the courtyard of the guard, the word of the LORD came to him a second time: "This is what the LORD says, he who made the earth, the LORD who formed it and established it—the LORD is his name: 'Call to me and I will answer you and tell you great and unsearchable things you do not know.'"

What I sensed God saying to me:

There is a Spirit world yet to be explored in your walk with me. Do not discount any dream or vision. Be brave, bold, and courageous as you share your Christian journey with others. You are not of this world—in the world but not of this world. You are a heavenly child of mine. The pain and suffering of this world will one day end. In the meantime, allow me to be your joy no matter what circumstances you are facing.

What message is God giving you?

_____

_____

_____

_____

_____

_____

_____

_____

_____

Conclude your month of listening in the dark places by meditating on the words of a song by Terry and Barbi Franklin. They apply the Old Testament story of Joseph and the New Testament account of Jesus to breaking our bondages and chains.

Prison to a Palace

It was deep and dark as night
And his body ached with pain
But deeper were the inner wounds
From his brother' cruel hate
He was sent so far away
Imprisoned as a slave
Where was all the meaning to his suffering?

Than one day they called his name
He was ushered to the King
And as he prayed for wisdom
The revelation came
They put a ring upon his hand
And appointed him to reign
How could this be happening so suddenly?

From a prison to a palace
Shackles to a throne
Where the reasons for life's seasons
Find meaning and you know
Your Heavenly Father's in control
And His loving hands all time and wisdom hold
When He lifts you from a prison to a palace.

There was yet another man
Whose shackled feet and hands
Were pierced for our transgressions
And by His wounds we're healed
He was obedient unto death
Then exalted to a throne
So that by His resurrection we can be set free

Breaking bondages and chains
In the power of Jesus name
To let us share the Kingly royalty
Is what the cross was for
He died to lift us from a

Prison to a palace
Shackles to a throne
Where the reasons for life's seasons
Find meaning, and you know
Your Heavenly Father's in control
And His loving hands all time and wisdom hold
When He lifts you from a prison to a palace.*
—Barbi and Terry Franklin

Barbi and Terry Franklin, "Prison to a Palace," *Go the Distance* (Nashville: Tylis Music Group/ASCAP, 1994). Administered by Gaither Copyright Management. Used by permission. www.heartfortheworld.com.

LISTENING IN THE SECRET PLACE

Although dreams mystify me, I suspect they come from hidden places in the mind. There have been times when I've taken my dreams to God and asked Him for insight into their meaning. Sometimes I sense He's giving me a message. Yet I broach this subject cautiously. I was crushed inwardly once by a lady who had dreamed an unpleasant dream about me and claimed her dreams were true. Jeremiah was brokenhearted by the messages of false prophets giving futile hope to the Israelites and leading them astray by claiming their messages were given to them in dreams by God. (See Jeremiah 23.) On the other hand, the Bible gives numerous examples of dreams that had significance.

In Genesis 37 the teenage Joseph had dreams that eventually came true. Years later, in Egypt, when Pharoah's chief cupbearer and baker had dreams in prison, Joseph explained both after saying, "Interpreting dreams is God's business" (Genesis 40:8, NLT).

God revealed King Nebuchadnezzar's dream to Daniel in a vision. When wise men in Nebuchadnezzar's kingdom were ordered killed because they could not interpret his troubling dream, Daniel gathered his friends Shadrach, Meshach, and Abednego and urged them to ask God to tell them the secret. "That night the secret was revealed to Daniel in a vision. Then Daniel praised the God of heaven" (Daniel 2:19, NLT).

In Daniel 7, Daniel—also called Belteshazzar—explained a dream with a frightening message to Nebuchadnezzar, and the dream was fulfilled. Throughout the Book of Daniel he had visions and wrote about his dreams. "Daniel had a dream and saw visions as he lay in his bed. He wrote down the dream" (v. 1). Daniel was terrified and kept the vision to himself. Three years later he had another vision. Gabriel came and explained the vision to Daniel and told him these things would not happen for a long time and to keep the vision a secret. Daniel was greatly troubled and became ill because of the vision. (See Daniel 8:15-27.)

During the first year of the reign of Darius the Mede, after reading from Jeremiah the prophet, Daniel prayed for his people, confessing his sin and that of the people. As he was praying, Gabriel came to give him insight. (See Daniel 9:1-20.)

As I was praying, Gabriel, whom I had seen in the earlier vision, came swiftly to me at the time of the evening sacrifice. He explained to me, "Daniel, I have come here to give you insight and understanding. The moment you began praying, a command was given. And now I am here to tell you what it was, for you are very precious to God. Listen carefully so that you can understand the meaning of your vision" *(Daniel 9:21-23, NLT)*.

Not only do we find accounts of dreams and visions in the Old Testament, but the first book of the New Testament gives several examples as well. The wise men were warned in a dream not to return to Herod with the message that they had found the Christ child but to travel home by another route. They obeyed. An angel appeared to Joseph in a dream telling him to take the child and his mother to Egypt. Joseph obeyed that very night. When Herod died, an angel appeared to Joseph again in a dream telling him to take his family back to the land of Israel. Joseph once again responded obediently. (See Matthew 2.)

Does God still speak today in visions and dreams? I don't know. However, I take to God the dreams that I remember and ask Him if He has something to reveal to me.

I've found myself recently praying in my dreams, and when I wake up I realize those were truly the prayers of my heart. I thank God that He heard my prayers and go back to sleep.

When I dream of someone I haven't seen or thought of for a long time, I awaken to pray for that individual and ask God to guide my prayers. Usually I go on a search to locate the person and ask if there are special ways I can pray for him or her.

When God brings someone to my mind to pray for, I wonder how many others he has called on to pray for that person also. Some general ways that I pray include for the person's protection, that he or she be safeguarded against temptations, and that his or her faith will be bolstered.

● ● ● ● ● ●

My friends Marilyn and Dave were packed and ready to leave Michigan for Dave to attend college in South Carolina when someone encouraged them to consider another college and provided a private plane for the visit if they would postpone their trip for a day.

Marilyn says, "Our plans were set for David to begin studies at another university funded by the GI Bill. We had our apartment rented and the U-Haul trailer hitched to our red Nash Rambler packed with our wedding gifts and everything else we owned. We were planning to leave the next morning."

David, a new Christian, postponed their travel and boarded the small aircraft to explore a place they knew nothing about. He came home enthusiastically, saying, "You can't believe what happened. God went before us and worked it all out. They accepted me as a student, I found an apartment for us, I have a job at the hospital, and you have a choice of two jobs at the bank."

Marilyn went to bed that night planning to give Dave a speech the next morning of all the reasons they should not change their original plans. That night Marilyn had a dream:

It was so peaceful. I was on a campus with a tree-lined street of tan brick apartment buildings. At the end of the street was a big red brick church with a white steeple. It was a contented sense of rightness and belonging—peace. God assured me, *This is right. Go. It will be all right.* When I awoke, the message and image were still vivid and real. I wanted to share the message God gave me through this dream, but I was not sure what my new Christian husband would think of my telling him that God had spoken to me. My plan to make my speech and have everything go my way became "It'll be all right—let's go."

When they arrived at the Illinois campus and were looking for the address of their new apartment, they turned onto a tree-lined street of tan brick apartment buildings across from a red brick church with a white steeple, where they made their home for the next seven years.

Exciting stories happened in that little brick home a few doors from the campus. Three daughters were born with May 16, 17, and 18 birthdays—all during David's final exam weeks. College takes longer when three babies come along, and Dave worked long hours so that Marilyn could stay at home with their daughters. Marilyn made Sunday dinner special with a lace tablecloth, pretty dishes, and the best meal of the week. Marilyn tells of one such Sunday:

I was standing at my sink washing dishes, looking through the mint green sheers blowing in the breeze. Suddenly and clearly, without warning, God spoke to me. *I want you to go to college.* I could not believe the message. It came again, clearly: *I want you to go to college.*

I responded quickly. *Who? Me? Surely not. You have the wrong person. You mean my husband. We're here for him to go to college. Look—he's in the living room reading his Russian history book. Besides, I'm not even college material, and we barely have money for him to go to college. By the way, did you forget that I have three babies? They're in there sleeping. Count them—one, two, three, all in one bedroom in this little four-room house.*

God's response was, *Go to the home economics house over there on Main Street and talk to the program director about starting your education here.*

Marilyn could see the building through the window and could not ignore this prompting any longer. Her story continues:

By faith, I dried my hands, took off my apron, and told David I was going for a short walk. As I climbed the steps to the front door of the big white building, I hoped no one would be there.

However, someone *was* there, and although that conversation is still fuzzy for Marilyn, that obedient act, along with the support of her husband, student babysitters, and a state grant, put her into the college arena as a student. Today Marilyn has a doctor of letters degree; has developed leadership programs; has been a bank president, college professor, pastor's wife, and chief financial officer of her denomination; and still listens to God's voice when He calls. You never know where God's dream will take you!

• • • • • •

The scripture readings this month remind us that only God can interpret dreams and reveal the secret places of the heart. Be hesitant to believe every story you hear, and never go off on a tangent reading and exploring the subject without scriptural and credible Christian guidance.

Use your dreams as an avenue of prayer to lift up to the Father those who appear in your dreams. He knows the need.

Focus for the Month:

Matthew 2
1 Corinthians 2
Jeremiah 2
Genesis 37-50
Daniel 3-6

TODAY IS _____

Listen through scripture:

JEREMIAH 23:9 AND 25-27, NLT:

My heart is broken because of the false prophets, and my bones tremble (23:9).

I have heard these prophets say, "Listen to the dream I had from God last night." And then they proceed to tell lies in my name. How long will this go on? If they are prophets, they are prophets of deceit, inventing everything they say. By telling these false dreams, they are trying to get my people to forget me, just as their ancestors did by worshiping the idols of Baal (23:25-27).

What I sensed God saying to me:

Guard against worshiping a style, plan, or idea. Keep the wonder of my creation alive. There will always be mystery in your encounters with me. I am God. You will never fully understand my ways. However, as you come to know me better and better, I will reveal hidden secrets to you. The awe of my presence and the praise in your heart grow greater as you accept this tremendous mystery. There is so much I still want to teach you, truths that will be impossible to verbalize to others. Each person must find his or her own way into my depths as he or she follows my call.

What message is God giving you?

_____

_____

_____

_____

_____

_____

_____

_____

TODAY IS _____

Listen through scripture:

JEREMIAH 23:16, NLT:

This is what the LORD of Heaven's Armies says to his people: "Do not listen to these prophets when they prophesy to you, filling you with futile hopes. They are making up everything they say. They do not speak for the LORD!"

What I sensed God saying to me:

In your dream last night you seemed to have lost your place. You were searching to find your way back to a comfortable spot. You were thinking that others were watching. You were amazed that this large church auditorium was packed, and you were wondering how a church of that size can be regularly filled with seekers. Let me tell you: churches can be filled for many reasons—not always the right reasons. If people see things happening that only I can do, they will come. However, some are coming only to watch, as did many who came to hear me speak and see me heal. Others will enjoy the overflow of those who are praying and obedient, but they will never surrender themselves to me. Do not assess my work by the crowds. Not every aspect of every dream has significance.

What message is God giving you?

_____

_____

_____

_____

_____

_____

_____

_____

TODAY IS _____

Listen through scripture:

JEREMIAH 23:21-22, NLT:

I have not sent these prophets, yet they run around claiming to speak for me. I have given them no message, yet they go on prophesying. If they had stood before me and listened to me, they would have spoken my words, and they would have turned my people from their evil ways and deeds.

What I sensed God saying to me:

I will help you sort through your dreams. You experienced many emotions during your dream last night—frustration, sadness that someone was troubled by something he or she thought you said that you do not even remember, your powerlessness to fix the problem and mend the relationship, your attempt to put it behind you so that you could face others in a positive manner, the wound to your spirit. You are wondering where this comes from. Use this experience to pray for your friends. You cannot control how others feel about what you say and do. You cannot fix or replace every negative thought or experience. You are right to try to redeem a damaged relationship, but then move ahead. Don't let it bind you or cause you to close your heart to future relationships. Don't let it spoil your next moment or adventure. Resolve to move ahead with a positive way in your world in spite of the troubling experience.

What message is God giving you?

_____

_____

_____

_____

_____

_____

_____

TODAY IS _____

Listen through scripture:

GENESIS 37:2-4, NLT:

This is the account of Jacob and his family. When Joseph was seventeen years old, he often tended his father's flocks. He worked for his half brothers, the sons of his father's wives Bilhah and Zilpah. But Joseph reported to his father some of the bad things his brothers were doing. Jacob loved Joseph more than any of his other children because Joseph had been born to him in his old age. So one day Jacob had a special gift made for Joseph—a beautiful robe. But his brothers hated Joseph because their father loved him more than the rest of them. They couldn't say a kind word to him.

What I sensed God saying to me:

Look at my Word now. Continue to look to me as a source of life, and I will make you like a well-watered garden. Keep this picture in your mind as you admire the beauty of my creation—green trees, flowering plants of all varieties clothed in splendor. Your African violet is reminding you to reach to me as your source of life as you observed its leaves and blossoms stretching upward. The bright purple blooms and the rich green leaves reveal that it has been properly watered and fed. Hold that image along with the one I gave you Saturday of my flashlight and umbrella as symbols of my guidance and protection. I want to give you more word pictures from Scripture—pictures that the heart remembers. When I send forth my Word, it produces fruit. It prospers everywhere I send it.

What message is God giving you?

_____

_____

_____

_____

_____

TODAY IS _____

Listen through scripture:

GENESIS 37:8, NLT:

His brothers responded, "So you think you will be our king, do you? Do you actually think you will reign over us?" And they hated him all the more because of his dreams and the way he talked about them.

What I sensed God saying to me:

Before you ever began reading the book on the life of a praying saint, I warned you that no two journeys are alike. He lived at a different time, in another country. He was a man on assignment by me. I am still using his life, as you can see. You, too, are on assignment by me, and I will continue to use your life after you are gone from this earth. However, your journey will only remotely resemble his. The places, events, and people will not be the same, but I will multiply your influence to generations beyond. The resemblance will come in the areas of self-giving, trust, listening to and obeying my voice, and empowerment to do the tasks I give you to do. You will witness dramatic answers to prayer that could come only from me.

What message is God giving you?

_____

_____

_____

_____

_____

_____

_____

_____

TODAY IS _____

Listen through scripture:

GENESIS 37:9-11, NLT:

Soon Joseph had another dream, and again he told his brothers about it. "Listen, I have had another dream," he said. "The sun, moon, and eleven stars bowed low before me!" This time he told the dream to his father as well as his brothers, but his father scolded him. "What kind of dream is that?" he asked. "Will your mother and I and your brothers actually come and bow to the ground before you?" But while his brothers were jealous of Joseph, his father wondered about what the dreams meant.

What I sensed God saying to me:

Ordinary days and weeks will come, and this is one. Yet no day in my presence, doing my will, serving me, is ordinary. "Surrender" is your word for today. Watch for it as you read and sing. Ponder it as you walk and work. Surrender your time, your schedule, your thoughts, your actions, your will, your emotions, your children, your husband, your home, your possessions, your future, your present, your tasks, your words, your all. Do not allow one iota of hypocrisy to reside in you.

What message is God giving you?

_____

_____

_____

_____

_____

_____

_____

_____

TODAY IS _____

Listen through scripture:

GENESIS 37:26-28, NLT:

Judah said to his brothers, "What will we gain by killing our brother? His blood would just give us a guilty conscience. Instead of hurting him, let's sell him to those Ishmaelite traders. After all, he is our brother—our own flesh and blood!" And his brothers agreed. So when the Ishmaelites, who were Midianite traders, came by, Joseph's brothers pulled him out of the cistern and sold him to them for twenty pieces of silver. And the traders took him to Egypt.

What I sensed God saying to me:

Give, contribute, donate! Start with your clothes. Move to your books. I will lead you from there as you sort and reorganize. Why would you choose to hold onto things you rarely wear or that are years old and no longer appealing or comfortable to you? Others have needs. Give things away while they are in good condition and have usefulness. This is all your own self-talk, but the concepts are prompted by me. You will feel lighter and happier after your giving spree.

What message is God giving you?

_____

_____

_____

_____

_____

_____

_____

_____

TODAY IS _____

Listen through scripture:

GENESIS 39:2-6, NLT:

The LORD was with Joseph, so he succeeded in everything he did as he served in the home of his Egyptian master. Potiphar noticed this and realized that the LORD was with Joseph, giving him success in everything he did. This pleased Potiphar, so he soon made Joseph his personal attendant. He put him in charge of his entire household and everything he owned. From the day Joseph was put in charge of his master's household and property, the LORD began to bless Potiphar's household for Joseph's sake. All his household affairs ran smoothly, and his crops and livestock flourished. So Potiphar gave Joseph complete administrative responsibility over everything he owned.

What I sensed God saying to me:

Your dream the other night reflected your cluttered mind. Your dream last night revealed more than meets the surface. It dealt with your regrets—regrets for lost opportunities, regrets of convictions you did not act upon, and the reality that you cannot go back and change your decisions. You are wrestling with your humanity. Give the burden to me. Go on from here.

What message is God giving you?

_____

_____

_____

_____

_____

_____

_____

_____

_____

TODAY IS _____

Listen through scripture:

GENESIS 41:1-16, NLT:

Two full years later, Pharoah dreamed that he was standing on the bank of the Nile River (v. 1).

But he fell asleep again and had a second dream (v. 5).

The next morning Pharoah was very disturbed by the dreams. So he called for all the magicians and wise men of Egypt. When Pharoah told them his dreams, not one of them could tell him what they meant. Finally, the king's chief cup-bearer spoke up (vv. 8-9).

Pharoah sent for Joseph at once, and he was quickly brought from the prison (v. 14).

Then Pharoah said to Joseph, "I had a dream last night, and no one can tell me what it means. But I have heard that when you hear about a dream you can interpret it."

"It is beyond my power to do this," Joseph replied. "But God can tell you what it means and set you at ease" (vv. 15-16).

What I sensed God saying to me:

I hear your desire to know truth and live in truth. A woman of truth will have no deceit, hypocrisy, guile, evil, misrepresentation, lie, or false nature. She will exemplify faithfulness, fidelity, honesty, constancy, character, sincerity, veracity, actuality, reality, and will not distort. I want you to be a veracious woman of God, marked by truth.

What message is God giving you?

_____

_____

_____

_____

_____

_____

TODAY IS _____

Listen through scripture:

GENESIS 41:57 AND 42:1-6, NLT:

People from all around came to Egypt to buy grain from Joseph because the famine was severe throughout the world (41:57).

When Jacob heard that grain was available in Egypt, he said to his sons, "Why are you standing around looking at one another? I have heard there is grain in Egypt. Go down there and buy enough grain to keep us alive. Otherwise we'll die." So Joseph's ten older brothers went down to Egypt to buy grain (42:1-3).

Since Joseph was governor of all Egypt and in charge of selling grain to all the people, it was to him that his brothers came. When they arrived, they bowed before him with their faces to the ground (42:6).

What I sensed God saying to me:

Sometimes to win is to lose. You have discovered that is true. Do not allow others to rob you of your joy. You can control your own thoughts and choices. You cannot make others patient, but you can cultivate patience in your own nature.

What message is God giving you?

_____

_____

_____

_____

_____

_____

_____

_____

TODAY IS _____

Listen through scripture:

GENESIS 45:24-28, NLT:

So Joseph sent his brothers off. . . . And they left Egypt and returned to their father, Jacob, in the land of Canaan.

"Joseph is still alive!" they told him. "And he is governor of all the land of Egypt!" Jacob was stunned at the news—he couldn't believe it. But when they repeated to Jacob everything Joseph had told them, and when he saw the wagons Joseph had sent to carry him, their father's spirits revived.

Then Jacob exclaimed, "It must be true! My son Joseph is alive! I must go and see him before I die."

What I sensed God saying to me:

Do not be disheartened when you do not hear clearly from me or what you do hear turns out differently than you expect. Living by faith makes you shaky at times. The greater your faith, the greater your sense of security will be.

What message is God giving you?

_____

_____

_____

_____

_____

_____

_____

_____

_____

TODAY IS _____

Listen through scripture:

GENESIS 46:1-5, NLT:

So Jacob set out for Egypt with all his possessions. And when he came to Beersheba, he offered sacrifices to the God of his father, Isaac. During the night God spoke to him in a vision. "Jacob! Jacob!" he called.

"Here I am," Jacob replied.

"I am God, the God of your father," the voice said. "Do not be afraid to go down to Egypt, for there I will make your family into a great nation. I will go with you down to Egypt, and I will bring you back again. But you will die in Egypt with Joseph attending to you."

So Jacob left Beersheba, and his sons took him to Egypt.

What I sensed God saying to me:

I am also doing a deep work in you, and I can be depended on to be faithful to complete it. You are on a quest for more spiritual knowledge. That hunger will be satisfied. You can be sure of this: I will be with you to the end, every step of the way.

What message is God giving you?

_____

_____

_____

_____

_____

_____

_____

_____

TODAY IS _____

Listen through scripture:

GENESIS 49:29; 50:12-22:

Then Jacob instructed them, "Soon I will die and join my ancestors. Bury me with my father and grandfather in the cave in the field of Ephron the Hitite" (49:29).

So Jacob's sons did as he had commanded them. They carried his body to the land of Canaan and buried him (50:12-13).

After burying Jacob, Joseph returned to Egypt with his brothers and all who had accompanied him to his father's burial. But now that their father was dead, Joseph's brothers became fearful. "Now Joseph will show his anger, and pay us back for all the wrong we did to him," they said (50:14-15).

But Joseph replied, "Don't be afraid of me. Am I God, that I can punish you? You intended to harm me, but God intended it all for good. He brought me to this position so I could save the lives of many people. No, don't be afraid, I will continue to take care of you and your children." So he reassured them by speaking kindly to them (50:19-21).

What I sensed God saying to me:

Meeting with me in the early-morning hours enables you to accomplish more for me. My heart is thrilled to meet with you and to share my thoughts with you.

What message is God giving you?

_____

_____

_____

_____

_____

_____

_____

TODAY IS _____

Read 1 Corinthians 2

Listen through scripture:

I CORINTHIANS 2:7-12, NLT:

No, the wisdom we speak of is the mystery of God—his plan that was previously hidden, even though he made it for our ultimate glory before the world began. But the rulers of this world have not understood it; if they had, they would not have crucified our glorious Lord. That is what the Scriptures mean when they say,

"No eye has seen, no ear has heard,
And no mind has imagine
What God has prepared for those who love him."

But it was to us that God revealed these things by his Spirit. For his Spirit searches out everything and shows us God's deep secrets. No one can know a person's thoughts except that person's own spirit, and no one can know God's thoughts except God's own Spirit. And we have received God's Spirit, not the world's spirit, so we can know the wonderful things God has freely given us.

What I sensed God saying to me:

You have taken on a job for yourself that I did not give you. I will help you this time, but learn from your impulsive decision. Carry out the task with love and prayer. Keep an open heart and sweet spirit. Watch and pray. Listen and pray. Awaken and pray. Go to sleep praying. Use the Sword of the Spirit as your weapon. Take courage. I am here.

What message is God giving you?

_____

_____

_____

_____

_____

TODAY IS _____

Listen through scripture:

I CORINTHIANS 2:13-16, NLT:

When we tell you these things, we do not use words that come from human wisdom. Instead, we speak words given to us by the Spirit, using the Spirit's words to explain spiritual truths. But people who aren't spiritual can't receive these truths from God's Spirit. It all sounds foolish to them and they can't understand it, for only those who are spiritual can understand what the Spirit means. Those who are spiritual can evaluate all things, but they themselves cannot be evaluated by others. For,

"Who can know the LORD's thoughts?
Who knows enough to teach him?"
But we understand these things, for we have the mind of Christ.

What I sensed God saying to me:

You are baffled by circumstances. Do not allow the inconsistencies of others to faze you. Do not respond with judgment toward those who do not cooperate. Do not take on the attitude of the apathetic ones. Keep your eyes above your surroundings, higher than your circumstances, on me rather than others. Walk on with boldness and courage.

What message is God giving you?

_____

_____

_____

_____

_____

_____

_____

Oswald Chambers wrote,

A secret silence means to shut the door deliberately on emotions and remember God. God is in secret, and He sees us from the secret place; He does not see us as other people see us, or as we see ourselves. When we live in the secret place it becomes impossible for us to doubt God, we become more sure of Him than of anything else. Your Father, Jesus says, is in secret and nowhere else. Enter the secret place, and right in the center of the common round you find God there all the time. Get into the habit of dealing with God about everything. Unless in the first waking moment of the day you learn to fling the door wide back and let God in, you will work on a wrong level all day; but swing the door wide open and pray to your Father in secret, and every published thing will be stamped with the presence of God.[1]

From the secret place, God sends us into His world to extend His grace.

LISTENING WHILE EXTENDING GRACE

Contemplation is an ancient spiritual discipline that has been practiced through the ages. Words God speaks to me during contemplative prayer and in my listening times are almost always private. Yet a few months ago He prompted me to write this book and reveal some of what I have sensed Him saying to me.

Contemplative prayer, in its simplest form, is prayer in which you still your thoughts and emotions and focus on God himself. This puts you in a better state to be aware of God's presence, and it makes you better able to hear God's voice correcting, guiding, and directing you. Instead of coming with a to-do list for God, you come with no agenda. The fundamental idea is simply to enjoy the companionship of God, stilling your own thoughts so you can listen should God choose to speak. For this reason, contemplative prayer is sometimes referred to as "the prayer of silence."[1]

Inner transformation takes place, and we leave the place of prayer feeling restored, at peace, and expecting to be surprised by God. "Those who practice contemplative prayer get used to waiting on God in expectant alertness. . . . The waiting is active—being fully present to each person and circumstance, convinced that God is on the move, wanting to be there to see what happens."[2]

As we leave our place of listening prayer, God sends us into a hurting world to extend His grace.

I rarely share with another person the words of discernment God gives me for fear that I'll give the pretense of being an authority from God. At times, however, He prompts me and gives me permission to reveal these insights.

A dear friend poured out her anguish to me regarding heartbreaking news from her daughter. In the night hours I was crying out to God with a broken spirit over this precious girl whom I had known since she was a small child. Early the next morning I wrote in my journal the words I sensed God speaking to me as His answer to my prayers. I later felt led to share those words with my friend: "I have heard your cries. I will deliver her. Watch for my miracle." It took a long time for the miracle of God's grace to unfold, and it's still ongoing. My friend often tells me how those words sustained her and her husband when it seemed they had not one shred of hope left.

Years later, I was preparing to speak at a pastors' wives retreat, and as I prayed for every lady, God gave me a word from Him for each one. I didn't think I would ever share those words with anyone, but during a quiet time at the retreat, I knew God was directing me to write a note to each of the ladies and share the message I had received regarding her. Little did I know that within a few months one of those ladies would face her daughter's death. These were His words:

> Darlene has walked with me faithfully and intimately for many years. I have brought her through deep waters numerous times along her journey with me. I am walking beside her, holding her hand. In the night hours as she sleeps, I am cradling her in my arms. I hear her heart cry and sobs for her children.

She told me that she reads that note often, and she has felt God's arms holding her many times. During her listening time at that retreat, God had reminded her to trust Him.

As the family drove away from the funeral home following her daughter's death, a stranger held out a sign to her from his vehicle that said, *Trust Jesus!* What a picture of grace extended!

God's children often bind up the wounded and serve Him, even while they're in the midst of pain and suffering of their own.

Terry, an internationally known songwriter and musician, recently told his story. He was raised in the home of unbelievers, and no one in his extended family attended church. One day two elderly ladies visited his home to invite the family to church.

Terry was the only one interested in going. One Sunday morning when he was acting up and disrupting the Sunday School class, the teacher took him into the hallway and sternly told him, "You are too good to act this way. I have been watching you, and God has his hand on your life. I expect you never to behave this way in class again."

Terry couldn't get the teacher's words out of his mind. It was a turning point for him, and today he and his wife have ministered around the world.

Terry adds that his teacher was serving in spite of an extremely painful family situation in his own life, yet he extended God's grace by teaching young men and giving discipline and affirming words that lodged in Terry's unruly young heart.

Jan Johnson says she often breathes a prayer, saying, *Show me this person's heart,* or she asks God, *What do I need to know about this person?*[3]

Stephen, the first Christian martyr, continued to extend grace and minister while enduring suffering. The 12 apostles decided they should spend their time teaching the Word of God and needed wise helpers full of the Spirit to care for the widows and distribute food. Stephen, a man full of faith and the Holy Spirit, was one of the seven chosen. (See Acts 6.) "Stephen, a man full of God's grace and power, performed amazing miracles and signs among the people" (v. 8, NLT).

Eventually, false accusations were made against Stephen, and he was arrested. His awesome address to the high priest and council summarized the story of the Jewish nation from Abraham, Joseph, Moses, King David, Solomon, all the way to the crucified and resurrected Jesus. They were infuriated when he boldly said they had deliberately disobeyed God's law and had betrayed and murdered the Messiah. (See Acts 7.)

But Stephen, full of the Holy Spirit, gazed steadily into heaven and saw the glory of God, and he saw Jesus standing in the place of honor at God's right hand. And he told them, "Look, I see the heavens opened and the Son of Man standing in the place of honor at God's right hand!" *(vv. 55-56).*

Stephen was dragged out of the city and stoned.

As they stoned him, Stephen prayed, "Lord Jesus, receive my spirit." He fell to his knees, shouting, "Lord, don't charge them with this sin!" And with that, he died *(vv. 59-60).*

I met another Stephen recently who is full of faith and the Holy Spirit, a man that God has called to extend His grace as a missionary. This Stephen, who had embraced the hippie lifestyle, was led to Jesus by a Christian who witnessed to him while he waited to attend a concert.

Stephen couldn't stop talking about Jesus and the Bible. He read the Gospel of John, was radically converted, and never looked back. His girlfriend, Laurie, now his wife, was not so easily persuaded. She had been raised in a family who attended church. She rebelled and was drawn to the hippie culture. By the time she was 16, she had fully embraced the clothes, music, cool boyfriend, drugs, and all. For several years she pursued a lifestyle of total rebellion. When a close friend was killed in a car accident, she began to study various religions and philosophies such as Hinduism,

Buddhism, and Shamanism, visited temples, attended meditation classes, and experimented with hallucinogenic drugs. After her boyfriend, Stephen, became a Christian, God tried to speak to her through music and people, but she resisted. Late one night she randomly opened the Bible to the Psalms and began reading the first chapter. She said that God began talking straight to her from His Word:

> He spoke to me about the stark contrast between a righteous lifestyle, which would be blessed and prosperous, and an ungodly lifestyle, which would perish. When I got to Psalm 5, He revealed to me that I was the wicked, deceitful work of iniquity that the Lord abhors. At the same time, He whispered sweet promises of joy, protection, and favor to those who loved His name. Oh, what an intense revelation I encountered through God's beautiful Word that night! I had many addictions and strongholds, so it took a few more months for me to totally surrender to Jesus, but when I did, there was such restoration. All the ropes of an ungodly life were cut. My dryness was saturated with the Living Water. I realized the truth by simply listening and obeying. I ended up marrying that radical Christian boyfriend, who is my best friend and mentor. We have four daughters and serve the Lord with gladness. I praise God for speaking to me in the past, and I praise Him for continuing to guide me now. I'm still listening.

Laurie has a dramatic story of how God called her to missions. When she shared with Stephen that God had spoken to her one day while rocking the baby, she found out that God had spoken to Stephen the night before, giving him an intense burden for missions and the lost. Now Laurie and Stephen are preparing to attend Bible college for the training they will need to extend God's grace in another country.

But we don't have to go to another country or even another neighborhood to extend grace. A few weeks ago a pastor I know said he was at the drive-through at Starbucks when the driver in front of him dilly-dallied so long after receiving his order that the waiting pastor became very impatient. Just as he started to blow his horn, the driver ahead moved forward. When the pastor attempted to pay for his coffee, the window attendant said, "No charge! Your bill was paid by the previous customer." My friend said that all the way to his destination God kept repeating, "Don't blow your horn—give coffee."

We've seen how God speaks not only through His Word but also through the testimony of others. How might God want to extend His grace through you today and tomorrow and next month and next year?

Rest assured that He has something to say *to* you and *through* you today if you simply listen. He may even use a phone call to extend His grace.

Rest Assured

Got another phone call
The same ole line or two
How's your family doin'
By the way, how are you?
You've been on my mind today
Just wanted you to know.
I've been on my knees liftin' your name to the throne

Rest assured He is with you every step of the way
Rest assured He will answer when you call on His Name
Tho' you're runnin' the last mile
Think you can't endure
He is right beside you
Rest assured

I paused for just a moment
Holdin' back the tears
What made you think of me
After all of these years?
If you'd heard the prayer I prayed
Before your call came through
I was on my knees
Cried, "Oh God please,
Could I hear from you?
I really need to hear from you.

I was listening for thunder
Or a mighty rushin' wind
Sometimes He speaks so clearly
Through the love of a friend
Yeh, Yeh
Rest assured He is with you every step of the way
Rest assured He will answer when you call on His Name
Tho' you're runnin' the last mile

Think you can't endure
He is right beside you
Rest assured.

—Elizabeth Shrum and Sheri Thrower

Elizabeth Shrum and Sheri Thrower, "Rest Assured," (Ringgold, Ga.: Sher-The-Music Publishing, BMI Inc.). Used by permission.

Focus for the Month:

Acts 3-16

TODAY IS _____

Read Acts 3

Listen through scripture:

ACTS 3:6-10:

Peter said, "Silver or gold I do not have, but what I have I give you. In the name of Jesus Christ of Nazareth, walk." Taking him by the right hand, he helped him up, and instantly the man's feet and ankles became strong. He jumped to his feet and began to walk. Then he went with them into the temple courts walking and jumping, and praising God. When all the people saw him walking and praising God, they recognized him as the same man who used to sit begging at the temple gate called Beautiful, and they were filled with wonder and amazement at what had happened to him.

What I sensed God saying to me:

Learn to concentrate on one task at a time and take breaks for relationships with others as well as with me. Not all of life has to be serious or work-related. Look at my life as an example. I took time to rest and to be alone. I made time for prayer and for celebrations. I was not always available to everyone who desired my attention. That is not only a human impossibility but is also not helpful to you or to those imposing on you.

What message is God giving you?

_____

_____

_____

_____

_____

_____

_____

TODAY IS _____

Read Acts 7

Listen through scripture:

ACTS 7:56-8:1:

"Look," he said, "I see heaven open and the Son of Man standing at the right hand of God." At this they covered their ears, and, yelling at the top of their voices, they all rushed at him, dragged him out of the city and began to stone him. Meanwhile, the witnesses laid their clothes at the feet of a young man named Saul. While they were stoning him, Stephen prayed, "Lord Jesus, receive my spirit." Then he fell on his knees and cried out, "Lord, do not hold this sin against them." When he had said this, he fell asleep. And Saul was there, giving approval to his death.

What I sensed God saying to me:

Touch your world through prayer. Do not give up. Even when your heart feels cold and prayerless, or when your schedule is filled with good things, stop and pray. Learn to pause for prayer every time someone makes a request of you or you are prompted to pray. Work and pray. Walk and pray. Watch and pray. Sit and pray. Stand and pray. Kneel and pray. Prayer is your lifeline to me.

What message is God giving you?

_____

_____

_____

_____

_____

_____

_____

TODAY IS _____

Read Acts 8

Listen through scripture:

ACTS 8:34-39:

The eunuch asked Philip, "Tell me, please, who is the prophet talking about, himself or someone else?" Then Philip began with that very passage of Scripture and told him the good news about Jesus. As they traveled along the road, they came to some water, and the eunuch said, "Look, here is water. Why shouldn't I be baptized?" And he gave orders to stop the chariot. Then both Philip and the eunuch went down into the water and Philip baptized him. When they came up out of the water, the Spirit of the Lord suddenly took Philip away, and the eunuch did not see him again, but went on his way rejoicing.

What I sensed God saying to me:

I am not calling you to fast now, but I will in the future. The call and purpose will be clear as well as the time and duration. Now you should care for your body in every way: exercising, eating nutritionally and on schedule, resting, and taking vitamins. Weight loss is not a reason to fast. Searching for some spiritual high is not a valid reason. Doing it because others say they do is not a good reason. Fast only when I lead you to. I am leading you at this time to care for your body and pray celebration prayers. Celebrate each time you eat. Don't pray only before your meals—pray after your meals as well.

What message is God giving you?

_____

_____

_____

_____

_____

TODAY IS _____

Read Acts 9

Listen through scripture:

ACTS 9:1:

Meanwhile, Saul was still breathing out murderous threats against the Lord's disciples. He went to the high priest and asked him for letters to the synagogues in Damascus, so that if he found any there who belonged to the Way, whether men or women, he might take them as prisoners to Jerusalem. As he neared Damascus on his journey, suddenly a light from heaven flashed around him. He fell to the ground and heard a voice say to him, "Saul, Saul, why do you persecute me?"

"Who are you, Lord?" Saul asked.

"I am Jesus, whom you are persecuting," he replied. "Now get up and go into the city, and you will be told what you must do."

What I sensed God saying to me:

You will never vanish from anyone's life forever. A piece of you is left behind everywhere you go. These times alone with me replenish you for your next encounter.

What message is God giving you?

_____

_____

_____

_____

_____

_____

_____

TODAY IS _____

Listen through scripture:

ACTS 14:1-3:

>   At Iconium Paul and Barnabas went as usual into the Jewish synagogue. There they spoke so effectively that a great number of Jews and Gentiles believed. But the Jews who refused to believe stirred up the Gentiles and poisoned their minds against the brothers. So Paul and Barnabas spent considerable time there, speaking boldly for the Lord who confirmed the message of his grace by enabling them to do miraculous signs and wonders.

What I sensed God saying to me:

>   No matter what others say or do, you are not to slander or even imply disrespectful or degrading thoughts about others. Do not allow the tone of your voice or your body language to be used to put others down—not in any way whatsoever. Ephesians 4:29-32 and Ephesians 4:1-2 are to be your guiding verses in this regard. Build others up in speech and actions.

What message is God giving you?

_____

_____

_____

_____

_____

_____

_____

_____

_____

_____

TODAY IS _____

Read Acts 16

Listen through scripture:

ACTS 16:9-15:

During the night Paul had a vision of a man of Macedonia standing and begging him, "Come over to Macedonia and help us." After Paul had seen the vision, we got ready at once to leave for Macedonia, concluding that God had called us to preach the gospel to them. . . . From there we traveled to Philippi. . . . On the Sabbath we went outside the city gate to the river, where we expected to find a place of prayer. We sat down and began to speak to the women who had gathered there. One of those listening was a woman named Lydia. . . . The Lord opened her heart to respond to Paul's message. When she and members of her household were baptized, she invited us to her home. "If you consider me a believer in the Lord," she said, "come and stay at my house." And she persuaded us.

What I sensed God saying to me:

Allow me to cover you with the dust of my sandals as you follow me closely and live by my teachings. "Goodness," "righteousness," and "truth" are your guide words.

What message is God giving you?

_____

_____

_____

_____

_____

_____

_____

_____

TODAY IS _____

Listen through scripture:

ROMANS 5:15, NLT:

There is a great difference between Adam's sin and God's gracious gift. For the sin of this one man, Adam, brought death to many. But even greater is God's wonderful grace and his gift of forgiveness to many through the other man, Jesus Christ.

What I sensed God saying to me:

Offer the parts of your body to me as instruments of righteousness, as mentioned in Romans 6:13:

- *Your mind: take every thought captive—read, learn, grow.*
- *Your mouth: speak boldly for me. Speak words of blessing to all.*
- *Your eyes: watch carefully. Look at others through my lens. Read the Word.*
- *Your ears: listen for me to speak. Hear the desperate cries around you.*
- *Your hands: touch others for me. Be my hands of comfort and blessing.*
- *Your arms: demonstrate affection. Wrap them around the world.*
- *Your feet: let me take you places you never dreamed you would go.*
- *Your heart: I will enlighten the eyes of your heart. Be obedient to the slightest directive from me.*

What message is God giving you?

_____

_____

_____

_____

_____

_____

_____

TODAY IS _____

Listen through scripture:

2 CORINTHIANS 4:13-18, NLT:

We continue to preach because we have the same kind of faith the psalmist had when he said, "I believed in God, so I spoke." We know that God, who raised the Lord Jesus, will also raise us with Jesus and present us to himself together with you. All of this is for your benefit. And as God's grace reaches more and more people, there will be great thanksgiving, and God will receive more and more glory. That is why we never give up. Though our bodies are dying, our spirits are being renewed every day. For our present troubles are small and won't last very long. Yet they produce for us a glory that vastly outweighs them and will last forever! So we don't look at the troubles we can see now, rather, we fix our gaze on things that cannot be seen. For the things we see now will soon be gone, but the things we cannot see will last forever.

What I sensed God saying to me:

My love cannot be bought, but it can be received. It cannot be sold, but it can be extended. Each day the life you lead proclaims the message of my love, and you bring my love to those who are lonely and afraid as you work with me to strengthen those who are in need.

What message is God giving you?

_____

_____

_____

_____

_____

_____

_____

_____

TODAY IS _____

Listen through scripture:

I TIMOTHY 1:15-17:

Here is a trustworthy saying that deserves full acceptance: Christ Jesus came into the world to save sinners—of whom I am the worst. But for that very reason I was shown mercy so that in me, the worst of sinners, Christ Jesus might display his unlimited patience as an example for those who would believe on and receive eternal life. Now to the King eternal, immortal, invisible, the only God, be honor and glory for ever and ever. Amen.

What I sensed God saying to me:

Here are some sacrifices I want you to make:

- *Watch carefully for individuals I send to cross your path. This will require discernment.*
- *Step out of your comfort zone to crumble walls, even when there are signs warning you to keep out. This will require courage.*
- *Forget your own self-interests. Go the second mile. This may cause you discomfort.*
- *Listen with open ears, a tender heart, penetrating eyes, and body language that says you're interested. This will require attentiveness.*
- *Speak only at my prompting, but do it with boldness.*
- *Do not avoid phone calls or people who tend to be annoying. Use every possible opportunity to spread my love to a broken, hurting world.*
- *Be generous with your time, money, and possessions.*

What message is God giving you?

_____

_____

_____

_____

_____

TODAY IS _____

Listen through scripture:

2 TIMOTHY 1:9-10, NLT:

God saved us and called us to live a holy life. He did this, not because we deserved it, but because that was his plan from before the beginning of time—to show us his grace through Christ Jesus. And now he has made all of this plain to us by the appearing of Christ Jesus, our Savior. He broke the power of death and illuminated the way to life and immortality through the Good News.

What I sensed God saying to me:

You have resolved to serve me all the days of your life. You continue to add burdens to your heart and place requirements on yourself: "Do this; do that." Before you know it, you have robbed yourself of the joy of doing, of obeying. Train yourself to relax in my presence, to rejoice in the doing, to refrain from placing restrictions on the way tasks are carried out. Take time to read without thinking, I should be doing . . . *Take time to walk without trying to pray, memorize, or do double duty. Just enjoy the walking, the reading, the resting.*

What message is God giving you?

_____

_____

_____

_____

_____

_____

_____

_____

TODAY IS _____

Listen through scripture:

TITUS 2:11-15:

The grace of God that brings salvation has appeared to all men. It teaches us to resist ungodliness and worldly passions and to live self-controlled, upright, and godly lives in this present age, while we wait for the blessed hope—the glorious appearing of our great God and Savior, Jesus Christ, who gave himself for us to redeem us from all wickedness and to purify for himself a people that are his very own, eager to do what is good. These, then, are the things you should teach.

What I sensed God saying to me:

I am near. Call on me. Seek my face. Give me your questions, your dreams, your failures. My mercy is everlasting. My grace is outpoured on you. You have been fully pardoned.

What message is God giving you?

_____

_____

_____

_____

_____

_____

_____

_____

_____

_____

_____

TODAY IS _____

Listen through scripture:

TITUS 3:3-8:

At one time we were foolish, disobedient, deceived and enslaved by all kinds of passions and pleasures. We lived in malice and envy being hated and hating one another. But when the kindness and love of God our Savior appeared, he saved us, not because of righteous things we had done, but because of his mercy. He saved us through the washing of rebirth and renewal by the Holy Spirit whom he poured out on us generously through Jesus Christ our Savior, so that, having been justified by his grace, we might become heirs having the hope of eternal life. This is a trustworthy saying. And I want you to stress these things, so that those who have trusted in God may be careful to devote themselves to doing what is good. These things are excellent and profitable for everyone.

What I sensed God saying to me:

Listen to me carefully today through scripture. Read with expectancy. My hands formed you, and I am still shaping you as I see best. Accept my molding, whether it is for a vessel for noble or for ordinary purposes. Yield to my hands. Let me have my own way with you. You are entering a new phase of molding. Remain pliable in my hands.

What message is God giving you?

_____

_____

_____

_____

_____

_____

_____

TODAY IS _____

Listen through scripture:

HEBREWS 4:12-16:

> *The word of God is living and active. Sharper than any double-edged sword, it penetrates even to dividing soul and spirit, joints and marrow; it judges the thoughts and attitudes of the heart. Nothing in all creation is hidden from God's sight. Everything is uncovered and laid bare before the eyes of him to whom we must give account. Therefore, since we have a great high priest who has gone through the heavens, Jesus the Son of God, let us hold firmly to the faith we profess. For we do not have a high priest who is unable to sympathize with our weaknesses, but we have one who has been tempted in every way, just as we are—yet was without sin. Let us then approach the throne of grace with confidence, so that we may receive mercy and find grace to help us in our time of need.*

What I sensed God saying to me:

Life is a treasure. Each day is my gift to you. Treat this gift with respect and wonder. Spend each day connecting with me and at least one of my children I place on your heart.

What message is God giving you?

_____

_____

_____

_____

_____

_____

_____

_____

TODAY IS _____

Listen through scripture:

JAMES 5:13-16:

Is any one of you in trouble? He should pray. Is anyone happy? Let him sing songs of praise. Is any one of you sick? He should call the elders of the church to pray over him and anoint him with oil in the name of the Lord. And the prayer offered in faith will make the sick person well; the Lord will raise him up. If he has sinned, he will be forgiven. Therefore confess your sins to each other and pray for each other so that you may be healed. The prayer of a righteous man is powerful and effective.

What I sensed God saying to me:

Be open. When you are exposed, do not resist. I am making you real. Responding as you think others want you to respond is not the answer. Changing your heart from inside out is the key. Often in the past you have performed as you perceived others expect you to perform in order to gain their approval. First of all, it is impossible to discern all the expectations of others—even when those expectations are expressed; the true feelings of others are not always exposed. Can you see how impossible this task is and what a burden it places on your performance? I have more to disclose to you on this subject.

What message is God giving you?

_____

_____

_____

_____

_____

_____

_____

TODAY IS _____

Listen through scripture:

ACTS 20:22-23:

And now, compelled by the Spirit, I am going to Jerusalem, not knowing what will happen to me there. I only know that in every city the Holy Spirit warns me that prison and hardships are facing me. However, I consider my life worth nothing to me, if only I may finish the race and complete the task the Lord Jesus has given me—that task of testifying to the gospel of God's grace.

What I sensed God saying to me:

Empty your cluttered mind when you come to me. I want to fill your heart and mind with my presence. I know it is unexplainable and beyond words to express. I reside in you. Feel my hand on your arm leading you. I am not only in you, but I also surround you. I am ahead, beckoning to you to come. I am behind, nudging you to new heights. I am beside you, leading and guiding. I am within you, loving and strengthening. I am above you, watching and protecting. I am beneath you, helping you carry your burdens. Satan has placed fear in your heart that does not belong there. Resist it. It will immobilize you. Keep your focus on me—your sustaining grace. My grace has covered your sin. My grace has purified and cleansed your heart. My grace is sufficient for you in all situations. Extend my grace.

What message is God giving you?

_____

_____

_____

_____

_____

_____

_____

Even if you are housebound or confined to bed, you can extend grace by interceding and praying for your family, church, community, state, country, and the nations. Join with others and pray big prayers—against the violence in our cities, the child abuse rampant everywhere, and the terrorism that abounds. Pray for godly parents, Spirit-filled pastors, political leaders with integrity, and God's glory to be revealed around the world. As you pray, however, remember to take time to simply listen and enjoy God's presence.

CONCLUSION

Do you find listening difficult? It seems as though everyone I ask answers in the affirmative.

Joseph Bentz poses this question in his book *Silent God:* "Is God too quiet, or is the world too noisy?"[1] He proposes that "Part of the function of noise in our lives is to keep us distracted from who we truly are. When that protective layer of chaos is stripped away and we find ourselves alone before God, we may not like the self who confronts us there."[2]

Bentz gives some very practical suggestions to reduce the noise, clutter, and agitation that block God's voice, yet there are times when we have eliminated the competing voices, gone to a quiet place, persevered in our attempts to hear God speak, and come away with nothing but silence! He makes an interesting point that perhaps God is silent until He has our attention. "We reach the place where we have nothing to rely on but Him alone. We face dangers during these painful periods, such as misinterpreting God's silence, turning to cynicism, or giving up on Him altogether. But when we hang on during these times, allowing Him to do His work, His presence comes flooding back, and we emerge not only more spiritually mature but also amazed at the surprising ways in which He carries out His design in us."[3]

Having said that, we know there are times when God speaks through the din and chaos of our world. He gets our attention in spite of all the clatter we surround ourselves with that might drown out His whispers.

I heard a former model tell her heartbreaking story with a joyful ending. At a noisy party, when her life had hit rock bottom, she looked around and said to herself, *These are the walking dead.* Her next thought was *And I'm one of them!* Those thoughts stuck in her mind and became a turning point. Today she is a pastor's wife, speaker, and powerful example of God's saving grace.

At a banquet I attended, a musician told of his rock band days when he was running from God. He said that one night from his position in the band, he looked around at bar scene that surrounded him. He heard a voice say, *You don't belong here.* He walked out in the middle of the song and never looked back. He now uses his talents around the country as a Christian artist.

One message from God can change the course of a life for eternity:
These are the walking dead, and you are one of them.
You don't belong here.
Turn around; do not go down that hill.
Take off your apron; I want you to go to college.
I've been watching you; God has His hand on your life.
Take off your sandals; you're on holy ground.
Leave your country and go to a place to which I will lead you.
Don't blow your horn; give coffee.
I will fill the empty hole in your heart.
I'm here; I'm all around you; I am everywhere.
Fear not, for I am with you.
I love you.
Trust Me.

Simply listen.

NOTES

Introduction

1. *The Spiritual Formation Bible* (Grand Rapids: Zondervan Publishing House, 1999), v-vi.

2. A. J. Russell, ed., *God Calling* (Urichsville, Oh.: Barbour Books, 1954).

Month 2

1. Earl Radmacher, Ron Allen, and H. Wayne House, *Compact Bible Commentary* (Nashville: Thomas Nelson, 2004), 7.

2. Ibid.

'3. Ibid.

4. Calvin Miller, *The Path of Celtic Prayer* (Downers Grove, Ill.: IVP Books, 2007), 24.

5. John Ortberg, *When the Game Is Over, It All Goes Back in the Box* (Grand Rapids: Zondervan Publishing House, 2007, 144.

6. Ibid.

Month 3

1. William Backus and Marie Chapian, *Telling Yourself the Truth* (Minneapolis: Bethany Fellowship Inc., 1980).

2. F. LaGard Smith, narrator, *The Narrated Bible in Chronological Order* (Eugene, Oreg.: Harvest House Publishers, 1984).

3. Miller, *The Path of Celtic Prayer*, 57.

Month 4

1. Smith, *The Narrated Bible in Chronological Order*, 97.

2. Ibid.

3. Jim Cymbala with Dean Merrill, *Fresh Wind, Fresh Fire* (Grand Rapids: Zondervan Publishing House, 1997), 25.

4. Ibid.

5. Ibid., 26.

6. Cymbala, *Fresh Wind, Fresh Fire*, 23-26.

7. Jan Johnson, *When the Soul Listens* (Colorado Springs: Navpress, 1999), 149.

Month 6

1. Miller, *The Path of Celtic Prayer*, 59.

Month 8

1. Pasty Lewis, *Simply Praying* (Kansas City: Beacon Hill Press of Kansas City, 2006).

2. Russell, *God Calling*.

3. Lewis, *Simply Praying*.

4. Jan Johnson, *Enjoying the Presence of God* (Colorado Springs: Navpress, 1996), 11.

5. Ibid., 92.

6. Ibid.

Month 9

1. Hannah Hurnard, *Hinds' Feet on High Places* (London: The Olive Press, 1955), 11-43.

2. Ibid., 52.

3. Ibid., 126.

4. Ibid., 143.

5. Ibid., 154-55.

Month 10

1. Dorie Van Stone with Erwin W. Lutzer, *Dorie: The Girl Nobody Loved* (Chicago: Moody Press, 1979).

2. Joseph Bentz, *Silent God* (Kansas City: Beacon Hill Press of Kansas City, 2007), 91.

3. Ibid.

4. Ibid.

5. Lewis, *Simply Praying*, 76.

6. Ibid.

Month 11

1. Oswald Chambers, *My Utmost for His Highest* (Urichsville, Oh.: Barbour, 1992), 172-73.

Month 12

1. Johnson, *When the Soul Listens*, 17.

2. Ibid., 106-107.

3. Ibid., 17.

Conclusion

1. Bentz, *Silent God*, 23.

2. Ibid., 81.

3. Ibid., 154.

BIBLIOGRAPHY

Backus, William, and Marie Chapian. *Telling Yourself the Truth*. Minneapolis: Bethany Fellowship Inc., 1980.

Bateman, Lana. *God's Crippled Children*. Dallas: Philippian Ministries, 1981.

Bentz, Joseph. *Silent God*. Kansas City: Beacon Hill Press of Kansas City, 2007.

Chambers, Oswald. *My Utmost for His Highest*. Urichsville, Oh.: Barbour and Company, Inc., 1992.

Cymbala, Jim, with Dean Merrill. *Fresh Wind, Fresh Fire*. Grand Rapids: Zondervan Publishing House, 1997.

Hurnard, Hannah. *Hinds' Feet on High Places* London: The Olive Press, 1955.

Johnson, Jan. *Enjoying the Presence of God*. Colorado Springs: Navpress, 1996.

———. *When the Soul Listens*. Colorado Springs: Navpress, 1999.

Lewis, Patsy. *Simply Praying*. Kansas City: Beacon Hill Press of Kansas City, 2006.

Ortberg, John. *When the Game Is Over, It all Goes Back in the Box*. Grand Rapids: Zondervan Publishing House, 2007.

Radmacher, Earl; Allen, Ron; and House, H. Wayne. *Compact Bible Commentary*. Nashville: Thomas Nelson, 2004.

Russell, A. J., ed. *God Calling*. Urichsville, Oh.: Barbour Books, 1954.

Smith, F. LaGard, narrator. *The Narrated Bible in Chronological Order*. Eugene, Oreg.: Harvest House Publishers, 1984.

The Spiritual Formation Bible. Grand Rapids: Zondervan Publishing House, 1999.

Van Stone, Dorie, with Erwin W. Lutzer. *Dorie: The Girl Nobody Loved*. Chicago: Moody Press, 1979.